RESEARCH METHODOLOGY:

AN EASY INTRODUCTION FOR THE BEGINNERS

MUBASHAR ALTAF

MERIT PUBLICATIONS ®

Lahore, Rawalpindi, Gujranwala . Ph: 0345-5218581, 0316-8028581

Copyright © 2019 MUBASHAR ALTAF

ISBN:
ISBN-13: 9781099213298

Price: 300

Dedication

TO MY CHILDREN, NAYYAB, FURQAN, AND FARYAB

ACKNOWLEDGMENTS

HERE I WANT TO SAY THANKS TO MY STUDENTS, FRIENDS AND FAMILY MEMBERS WHO HELPED ME A LOT TO COMPLETE THIS HECTIC TASK OF WRITING RESEARCH METHODOLOGY

PREFACE

This book is based upon my experiences in research as a student, practitioner, and teacher. The difficulties I faced in understanding research as a student, my discoveries about what was applicable and inapplicable in the field as a practitioner, and my development of the ability effectively to communicate difficult concepts in simple language without sacrificing technicality and accuracy as a teacher has become the basis of this book.

The research methodology is taught as a supporting subject in several ways in many academic disciplines such as health, education, psychology, social work, nursing, public health, library studies, English studies, and marketing research. The core philosophical base for this book comes from my conviction that, although these disciplines vary in content, their broad approach to a research inquiry is similar. This book, therefore, is addressed to these academic disciplines.

It is true that some disciplines place greater emphasis on quantitative research and some on qualitative research. My own approach to research is a combination of both. Firstly, it is the objective that should decide whether a study be carried out adopting a qualitative or a quantitative approach. Secondly, in real life, most research is a combination of both methods. Though they differ in the philosophy that underpins their mode of inquiry, to a great extent their broad approach to inquiry is similar. The quantitative research process is reasonably well structured whereas the qualitative one is fairly unstructured, and these are their respective strengths as well as weaknesses. I strongly believe that both are important to portray a complete picture. In addition, there are aspects of quantitative research that are qualitative in nature. It depends on how a piece of information has been collected and analyzed. Therefore I feel very strongly that a good researcher needs to have both types of skills. I follow a qualitative–quantitative-qualitative approach to an inquiry. This book, therefore, has been written to provide theoretical information in an operational manner about methods, procedures, and techniques that are used in both approaches.

Research as a subject is taught at different levels. The book is designed specifically for students who are newcomers to research and who may have a psychological barrier with regard to the subject.

I have therefore not assume any previous knowledge on the part of the reader; I have omitted detailed discussion of aspects that may be inappropriate for beginners; I have used many flow charts and examples to communicate concepts, and areas covered in the book follow a 'simple to complex' approach in terms of their discussion and coverage.

The structure of this book, which is based on the model developed during my teaching career, is designed to be practical. The theoretical knowledge that constitutes research methodology is therefore organized around the operational steps that form this research process for both quantitative and qualitative research. All the information needed to take a particular step, during the actual research journey, is provided in one place. The needed information is organized in chapters and each chapter is devoted to a particular aspect of that step.

It is my belief that a sound knowledge of research methodology is essential for undertaking a valid study. To answer your research questions, 'Writing a research proposal', knowledge of research methods is crucial as this enables you to develop a conceptual framework that is sound and has merits for undertaking your research endeavor with confidence. Having completed the preparatory work, the steps that follow are more practical in nature, the quality of which entirely depends upon the soundness of the methodology you proposed in your research proposal. Statistics and computers play a significant role in the research but their application is mainly after the data has been collected. To me, statistics are useful in confirming or contradicting conclusions drawn from simply looking at analyzed data, in providing an indication of the magnitude of the relationship between two or more variables under study, in helping to establish causality, and in ascertaining the level of confidence that can be placed in your findings. A computer's application is primarily in data analysis, the calculation of statistics, word processing and the graphic presentation of data. It saves time and makes it easier for you to undertake these activities; however, you need to learn this additional skill. This book does not include statistics or information about computers.

MUBASHAR ALTAF   **18 MAY 2019**

CONTENTS

The page is left blank intentionally

TOPIC
01

What is Research?

The Sapiens want to grip their environment and to understand nature through experience, reasoning, and research.

RESEARCH is a Systematic, controlled, empirical & critical investigation of hypothetical propositions about the presumed relations among natural phenomena, I.e., Systematic & controlled Empirical Self-correcting Research is a combination of both experience & reasoning and must be regarded as the most successful approach to the discovery of truth (particularly in natural sciences)

❖ **Research** is a voyage of discovery; a journey; an attitude; an experience; a method of critical thinking; a careful critical inquiry in seeking facts for principles.

❖ An art of scientific investigation

❖ A scientific and systematic search for pertinent information on a specific topic

❖ Process of arriving at dependable solutions to problems through the planned and systematic collection, analysis and interpretation of data

❖ A systematized effort to gain new knowledge; a movement from the known to the unknown

❖ Search for (new) knowledge/ facts through objective, systematic and scientific method of finding a solution to a problem

❖ Implicit question + Explicit answer + data to answer the question

❖ Not synonymous with common sense, but systematic, objective (purposeful), reproducible, relevant activity

having control over some factors

An activity caused by the instinct of inquisitiveness to gain fresh insight / find answers to question/acquire knowledge In a broad sense, everyone does research, but don't write it up; Without trustworthy and tested published research available we are dangerously lost in the experience, opinions, and hearsay

WHY RESEARCH?

- ❖ To get a degree
- ❖ To get respectability
- ❖ To face a challenge
- ❖ To solve a problem
- ❖ To get intellectual joy
- ❖ To serve society

Benefits of Research Methodology

- ❖ Advancement of the wealth of human knowledge `
- ❖ Provides tools to look at things in life objectively
- ❖ Develops a critical and scientific attitude, disciplined thinking or a 'bent of mind' to observe objectively (scientific deduction & inductive thinking); Skills of research will pay-off in long term particularly in the 'age of information' (or too often of misinformation)
- ❖ Enriches practitioner and his practices; Provides a chance to study a subject in depth; Enable us to make intelligent decisions; Understand the material which no other kind of work can match
- ❖ As consumers of research output help to inculcate the ability to evaluate and use the results of earlier research with reasonable confidence and take rational decisions. Doing research is the best way to learn to read and think critically
- ❖ Additional benefits in the case of librarianship: i. helps to understand the 'researcher' as a user of the library and Helps to learn how to use libraries & other information resources
- ❖ Enables critical evaluation of literature
- ❖ Develops special interests & skills. It helps to understand the attitude of others. It creates

awareness of the special needs of the research process.

ARISTOTLE'S METHOD OF THE PRODUCTION OF NEW KNOWLEDGE

When Aristotle was asked, "how do you create new knowledge", he replied "I follow a method/process to create/ produce new knowledge"

1. **I STUDY THE PRIOR/PREVIOUS IDEAS/ KNOWLEDGE ABOUT THE SUBJECT** (IN MODERN TERMS, LITERATURE REVIEW)
2. **THEN I FIND THE CONTRACTION/ DIALECTICS** (OPPOSING THOUGHTS/IDEAS, OR IN MODERN TERMS PROBLEM, CONTENTION, QUESTION)
3. **THEN I APPLY LOGIC** (INDUCTION OR DEDUCTION) (IN MODERN TERMS, DATA ANALYSIS)
4. **AFTER ANALYSIS WHAT I FIND IS NEW KNOWLEDGE, WHICH I CALL SCIENCE** (IN MODERN TERMS, FINDINGS/CONCLUSION)

TOPIC
02

RESEARCH METHODOLOGY & PREVIOUS SOURCES OF KNOWLEDGE

Take a minute to ponder some of what you know and how you acquired that knowledge. Perhaps you know that you should make your bed in the morning because your mother or father told you this is what you should do; perhaps you know that crows are black because all of the crows you have seen are black. But should we trust knowledge from these sources? Before RM the methods of acquiring knowledge can be broken down into five categories each with its own strengths and weaknesses.

1.   TRADITION & SOCIAL CUSTOMS

Most of the things and doings we do and have come from tradition. The ceremony of birth, death, and marriage are traditional. We do many things learned from our tradition unquestionably.

2.   AUTHORITY

Perhaps one of the most common methods of acquiring knowledge is through authority. This method involves accepting new ideas because some authority figure states that they are true. These authorities include parents, the media, doctors, Priests and other religious authorities, the government, and professors. While in an ideal world we should be able to trust authority figures, history has taught us otherwise and many instances of atrocities against humanity are a consequence of people unquestioningly following authority (e.g., Salem Witch Trials, Nazi War Crimes). On a more benign level, while your parents may have told you that you should make your bed in the morning, making your bed provides a warm damp environment in which mites thrive. Keeping the sheets open provides a less hospitable environment for mites. These examples illustrate that the problem with using authority to obtain knowledge is that they may be wrong, they may just be using their intuition to arrive at their conclusions, and they may have their own reasons to mislead you. Nevertheless, much of the information we acquire is through authority because we don't have time to question and independently research every piece of knowledge we learn through authority. But we can learn to evaluate the credentials of authority figures, to evaluate the methods they used to arrive at their conclusions, and evaluate whether they have any reasons to mislead us.

3.   **INTUITION**

The third method of knowing is intuition. When we use our intuition, we are relying on our guts, our emotions, and/or our instincts to guide us. Rather than examining facts or using rational thought, intuition involves believing what feels true. The problem with relying on intuition is that our intuitions can be wrong because they are driven by cognitive and motivational biases rather than logical reasoning or scientific evidence. While the strange behavior of your friend may lead you to think s/he is lying to you it may just be that s/he is holding in a bit of info or is preoccupied with some other issue that is irrelevant to you. However, weighing alternatives and thinking of all the different possibilities can be paralyzing for some people and sometimes decisions based on intuition are actually superior to those based on analysis (people interested in this idea should read Malcolm Gladwell's book *Blink*).

4.   **REVELATION**

We are told that in ancient times God directly revealed his commands and knowledge to the heart of the chosen ones. But the basic problem with this source of knowledge is that we cannot verify the source or method of acquisition and moreover everyone is not the chosen one. We are common people we need a common method which we can learn and teach. We can verify through our ordinary senses. So revelation cannot be taught in the institution to everyone

5.   **MAGIC**

In ancient times and in some areas still, people believe in magic. Some think that it is a great source of knowledge especially an evil kind of knowledge. But the problem with this source is that we cannot verify the source and actions. Modern experiments show that magic means only an illusion of senses. It is based on the deception of senses.

TOPIC

03

SCIENTIFIC METHOD OF RESEARCH & ITS SPECIAL FEATURES

Research produces knowledge that could be used for the solution of problems as well as for the generation of universal theories, principles, and laws. But all knowledge is not science. The critical factor that separates scientific knowledge from other ways of acquiring knowledge is that it uses a scientific approach. **What is this approach? Or what is science?**

When most people hear the word *science*, the first image that comes to mind is one of the test tubes, computers, rocket ships, and people in white lab coats. These outward trappings are part of science.

Some sciences, such as the natural sciences deal with the physical and material world. Some other sciences involve the study of people – their beliefs, behavior, interactions, attitudes, institutions, and so forth. They are sometimes called *soft sciences*. This is not that their work is sloppy or lack rigor but because their subject matter, human social life, is fluid, formidable to observe, and hard to measure precisely with laboratory instruments. The subject matter of a science (e.g. human attitudes, protoplasm, or galaxies) determines the techniques and instruments (e.g. surveys, microscopes, or telescopes) used by it.

Science is a way to produce knowledge, which is based on truth and attempts to be universal. In other words, science is a method, a procedure to produce knowledge i.e. discovering universalities/principles, laws, and theories through the process of observation and re-observation. The observation here implies that scientists use "sensory experiences" for the study of the phenomena. They use their five senses, which are possessed by every normal human being. They not only do the observation of a phenomenon but also repeat the observation, maybe several times. The researchers do so because they want to be accurate and definite about their findings

Re-observation may be made by the same researcher at a different time and place or done by other professionals at some other time or place. All such observations are made in this universe where a normal professional human being can go, make the observation and come back. Therefore we are focusing on this universe, not on the one hereafter. By repeating the observation, the researchers want to be definite and positive about their findings. Those who want to be definite and positive are often referred to as **positivists**. The researchers do not leave their findings into scattered bits and pieces.

Rather the results are organized, systematized, and made part of the existing body of knowledge; and this is how the knowledge grows. All this procedure for the creation of knowledge is called a scientific method, whereby the consequent knowledge may be referred to as scientific knowledge. In this way, *science* refers to both a system for producing knowledge and the knowledge produced from that system. Since the subject matters of the researchers differ, therefore, we have the diversification of different sciences: broadly natural or physical sciences and human sciences.

Important Characteristics of Scientific Method/Research Method

1. Empirical

The scientific method is concerned with the realities that are observable through "**sensory experiences.**" It generates knowledge that is verifiable by experience or observation. Some of the realities could be directly observed, like the number of students present in the class and how many of them are male and how many females. The same students have attitudes, values, motivations, aspirations, and commitments.

These are also realities that cannot be observed directly, but the researchers have designed ways to observe these indirectly. Any reality that cannot be put to "sensory experience" directly or indirectly (existence of heaven, the Day of Judgment, life hereafter, God's rewards for good deeds) does not fall within the domain of scientific method.

2.   Verifiable

Observations made through the scientific method are to be verified again by using the senses to confirm or refute the previous findings. Such confirmations may have to be made by the same researcher or others.

We will place more faith and credence in those findings and conclusions if similar findings emerge on the basis of data collected by other researchers using the same methods. To the extent that it does happen (i.e. the results are replicated or repeated), we will gain confidence in the scientific nature of our research. **Replicability**, in this way, is an important characteristic of the scientific method. Hence revelations and intuitions are out of the domain of scientific method.

3.   Cumulative

Prior to the start of any study, the researchers try to scan through the literature and see that their study is not a repetition in ignorance. Instead of reinventing the wheel the researchers take stock of the existing body of knowledge and try to build on it. Also, the researchers do not leave their research findings into scattered bits and pieces. Facts and figures are to be provided with language and thereby inferences are drawn. The results are to be organized and systematized. Nevertheless, we don't want to leave our studies as a standalone. A linkage between the present and the previous body of knowledge has to be established, and that is how the knowledge accumulates. Every new crop of babies does not have to start from scratch; the existing body of knowledge provides a huge foundation on which the researchers build on and hence the knowledge keeps on growing.

4.   Deterministic

Science is based on the assumption that all events have antecedent causes that are subject to identification and logical understanding. For the scientist, nothing "just happens" – it happens for a reason. The scientific researchers try to explain the emerging phenomenon by identifying its causes. Of the identified causes which ones can be the most important? For example, in the 2019 BS examination of Sargodha University, 67 percent of the students failed. What could be the determinants of such a mass failure of students? The researcher may try to explain this phenomenon and come up with a variety of reasons which may pertain to students, teachers, administration, curriculum, books, examination system, and so on. Looking into such a large number of reasons may be a highly cumbersome model for problem-solving. It might be appropriate to tell, of all these factors which one is the most important, the second most important, the third most important, which two in combination are the most important. The researcher tries to narrow down the number of reasons in such a way that some action could take. Therefore, the achievement of a meaningful, rather than an elaborate and cumbersome, model for problem solution becomes a critical issue in research. That is parsimony which implies the explanation with the minimum number of variables that are responsible for an undesirable situation.

5.   Ethical and Ideological Neutrality

The conclusions drawn through the interpretation of the results of data analysis should be objective; that is, they should be based on the facts of the findings derived from actual data, and not on our own subjective or emotional values. For instance, if we had a hypothesis that stated that greater participation in decision making will increase organizational commitment, and this was not supported by the results, it makes no sense if the researcher continues to argue that increased opportunities for employee participation would still help. Such an argument would be based, not on the factual, data-based research findings, but on the subjective opinion of the researcher. If this was the conviction of the researcher all along, then there was no need to do the research in the first place.

Researchers are human beings, having individual ideologies, religious affiliations, cultural differences which can influence the research findings. Any interference of their personal likings and dis-likings in their research can contaminate the purity of the data, which ultimately can affect the predictions made by the researcher. Therefore, one of the important characteristics of the scientific method is to follow the principle of objectivity, uphold neutrality, and present the results in an unbiased manner.

6.   Generalization

Generalizability refers to the scope of the research findings in one organizational setting to other settings.

Obviously, the wider the range of applicability of the solutions generated by research, the more useful the research is to users. For instance, if a researcher's findings that participation in decision making enhances organizational commitment are found to be true in a variety of manufacturing, industrial, and service organizations, and not merely in the particular organization studied by the researcher, the generalizability of the findings to other organizational settings is enhanced. The more generalizable the research, the greater its usefulness and value.

For wider generalizability, the research sampling design has to be logically developed and a number of other details in the data collection methods need to be meticulously followed. Here the use of statistics is very helpful. Statistics is a device for comparing what is observed and what is logically expected. The use of statistics becomes helpful in making generalizations, which is one of the goals of the scientific method.

7.   Rationalism

Science is fundamentally a rational activity, and the scientific explanation must make sense. Religion may rest on revelations, customs, or traditions, gambling on faith, but science must rest on logical reason.

There are two distinct logical systems important to the scientific quest, referred to as deductive logic and inductive logic. Beveridge describes them as follows:

*Logicians distinguish between **inductive reasoning** (from particular instances to general principles, from facts to theories) and **deductive reasoning** (from the general to the particular, applying a theory to a particular case). In induction, one starts from observed data and develops a generalization that explains the relationships between the objects observed. On the other hand, in deductive reasoning one starts from some general law and applies it to a particular instance.*

The classical illustration of deductive logic is the familiar **syllogism**: "All men are mortal; Mahmoud is a man; therefore Mahmoud is mortal." A researcher might then follow up this deductive exercise with an empirical test of Mahmoud's mortality.

Using inductive logic, the researcher might begin by noting that Mahmoud is mortal and observing a number of other mortals as well. He might then note that all the observed mortals were men, thereby arriving at the tentative conclusion that all men are mortal.

In practice, scientific research involves both inductive and deductive reasoning as the scientist shifts endlessly back and forth between theory and empirical observations.

There could be some other aspects of the scientific method (e.g. self-correcting) but what is important is that

All features are interrelated.

Scientists may not adhere to all these characteristics. For example, objectivity is often violated especially in the study of human behavior, particularly when human beings are studied by human beings. Personal biases of the researchers do contaminate the findings.

Looking at the important features of scientific method one might say that there are

Two power bases of scientific knowledge:

(1) *empiricism* i.e. sensory experiences or observation, and

(2) *Rationalism* i.e. the logical explanations for regularity and then consequent argumentation for making generalizations (theory).

Finally, it may be said that anybody who is following the scientific procedure of doing research is doing scientific research, and the knowledge generated by such research is scientific knowledge. Depending upon the subject matter, we try to divide the sciences into physical or natural sciences and the social sciences. Due to the nature of the subject matter of the social sciences, it is rather very difficult to apply the scientific method of research rigorously and that is why the predictions made by the social researchers are not as dependable as the predictions made by the natural scientists.

SCIENCE VERSUS PSEUDOSCIENCE

Pseudoscience refers to activities and beliefs that are claimed to be scientific by their proponents—and may appear to be scientific at first glance—but are not.

Consider the theory of biorhythms (not to be confused with sleep cycles or circadian rhythms that do have a scientific basis). The idea is that people's physical, intellectual, and emotional abilities run in cycles that begin when they are born and continue until they die. Allegedly, the physical cycle has a period of 23 days, the intellectual cycle a period of 33 days, and the emotional cycle a period of 28 days. So, for example, if you had the option of when to schedule an exam, you would want to schedule it for a time when your intellectual cycle will be at a high point. The theory of biorhythms has been around for more than 100 years, and you can find numerous popular books and websites about biorhythms, often containing impressive and scientific-sounding terms like *sinusoidal wave* and *bioelectricity*. The problem with biorhythms, however, is that scientific evidence indicates they do not exist (Hines, 1998).

The word **pseudoscience** literally means **"false science"**. **Creationism, alchemy, alternative medicine** and **astrology** are well-known pseudosciences.

TOPIC
04

CLASSIFICATION OF RESEARCH

The research comes in many shapes and sizes. Before a researcher begins to conduct a study, he or she must decide on a specific type of research. Good researchers understand the advantages and disadvantages of each type, although most end up specializing in one.

For the classification of research we shall look from four dimensions:

1.   The purpose of doing research

2.   The intended uses of research

3.   How it treats time i.e. the time dimension in research

4.   The research (data collection) techniques used in it

The four dimensions reinforce each other; that is, a purpose tends to go with certain techniques and particular uses. Few studies are pure types, but the dimensions simplify the complexity of conducting research.

1. Types According to the Purpose of Doing Research

If we ask someone why he or she is conducting a study, we might get a range of responses: "My boss told me to do"; "It was a class assignment"; "I was curious." There are almost as many reasons to do research as there are researches. Yet the purposes of research may be organized into three groups based on what the researcher is trying to accomplish – explore a new topic, describe a social phenomenon, or explain why something occurs. Studies may have multiple purposes (e.g. both to explore and to describe) but one purpose usually dominates.

a.   Exploratory/Formative Research

You may be **exploring a new topic** or issue in order to learn about it. If the issue was new or the researcher has written little on it, you began at the beginning. This is called *exploratory research.* The researcher's goal is to formulate more precise questions that future research can answer. Exploratory research may be the first stage in a sequence of studies. A researcher may need to know enough to design and execute a second, more systematic and extensive study.

Initial research conducted to clarify the nature of the problem. When a researcher has a limited amount of experience with or knowledge about a research issue, **exploratory research** is a useful preliminary step that helps ensure that a more rigorous, more conclusive future study will not begin with an inadequate understanding of the nature of the management problem. The findings discovered through exploratory research would the researchers to emphasize learning more about the particulars of the findings in subsequent conclusive studies.

Exploratory research rarely yields definitive answers. It addresses the "what" question: "what is this social activity really about?" It is difficult to conduct because there are few guidelines to follow.

Specifically, there could be a number of goals of exploratory research.

Goals of Exploratory Research

1. Become familiar with the basic facts, setting, and concerns;
2. Develop a well-rounded picture of the situation;
3. Develop tentative theories; generate new ideas, conjectures, or hypotheses;
4. Determine the feasibility of conducting the study;
5. Formulate questions and refine issues for more systematic inquiry; and
6. Develop techniques and a sense of direction for future research.

    For exploratory research, the researcher may use
    different sources for getting information like
(1) Experience surveys,
(2) Secondary data analysis,
(3) Case studies, and

(4)   Pilot studies.

As part of the experience survey, the researcher tries to contact individuals who are knowledgeable about a particular research problem. This constitutes an informal experience survey.

Another economical and quick source of background information is secondary data analysis. It is a preliminary review of data collected for another purpose to clarify issues in the early stages of a research effort.

The purpose of the case study is to obtain information from one or a few situations that are similar to the researcher's problem situation. A researcher interested in doing a nationwide survey among union workers may first look at a few local unions to identify the nature of any problems or topics that should be investigated.

A pilot study implies that some aspect of the research is done on a small scale. For this purpose, focus group discussions could be carried out.

b.   Descriptive Research

Descriptive research presents a picture of the specific details of a situation, social setting, or relationship. The major purpose of descriptive research, as the term implies, is to describe characteristics of a population or phenomenon. Descriptive research seeks to determine the answers to *who, what, when, where*, and *how* questions. Labor Force Surveys, Population Census, and Educational Census are examples of such research. The descriptive study offers to the researcher a profile or description of relevant aspects of the phenomena of interest. Look at the class in research methods and try to give its profile – the characteristics of the students. When we start to look at the relationship between the variables, then it may help in diagnosis analysis.

Goals of Descriptive Research

1.   Describe the situation in terms of its characteristics i.e. provide an accurate profile of a group;
2.   Give a verbal or numerical picture (%) of the situation;
3.   Present background information;
4.   Create a set of categories or classify the information;

5.　　Clarify sequence, set of stages; and

6.　　Focus on 'who,' 'what,' 'when,' 'where,' and 'how' but not why?

A great deal of social research is descriptive. Descriptive researchers use most data –gathering techniques – surveys, field research, and content analysis

c.　Explanatory Research

When we encounter an issue that is already known and have a description of it, we might begin to wonder *why* things are the way they are. The desire to know "why," to explain, is the purpose of *explanatory research*. It builds on exploratory and descriptive research and goes on to identify the reasons for something that occurs. Explanatory research looks for causes and reasons. For example, descriptive research may discover that 10 percent of the parents abuse their children, whereas the explanatory researcher is more interested in learning *why* parents abuse their children.

Goals of Explanatory Research

1.　　Explain things not just reporting.

2.　　Why?

3.　　Elaborate and enrich a theory's explanation.

4.　　Determine which of several explanations is best.

5.　　Determine the accuracy of the theory; test a theory's predictions or principles.

6.　　Advance knowledge about the underlying process.

7.　　Build and elaborate a theory; elaborate and enrich a theory's predictions or principles.

8.　　Extend a theory or principle to new areas, new issues, new topics:

9.　　Provide evidence to support or refute an explanation or prediction.

10.　　Test a theory's predictions or principles

2. Types According to the Intended Uses of the Research

Some researchers focus on using research to advance general knowledge, whereas others use it to solve specific problems. Those who seek an understanding of the fundamental nature of social reality are engaged in basic research (also called academic research or pure research or fundamental research).

Applied researchers, by contrast, primarily want to apply and tailor the knowledge to address a specific practical issue. They want to answer a policy question or solve a pressing social and economic problem.

a.   Basic Research

Basic research advances fundamental knowledge about the human world. It focuses on refuting or supporting theories that explain how this world operates, what makes things happen, why social relations are a certain way, and why society changes. Basic research is the source of most new scientific ideas and ways of thinking about the world. It can be exploratory, descriptive, or explanatory; however, explanatory research is the most common.

Basic research generates new ideas, principles, and theories, which may not be immediately utilized; though are the foundations of modern progress and development in different fields. Today's computers could not exist without the pure research in mathematics conducted over a century ago, for which there was no known practical application at that time. Police officers trying to prevent delinquency or counselors of youthful offenders may see little relevance to basic research on the question, "Why does deviant behavior occur?" Basic research rarely helps practitioners directly with their everyday concerns. Nevertheless, it stimulates new ways of thinking about deviance that have the potential to revolutionize and dramatically improve how practitioners deal with a problem. A new idea or fundamental knowledge is not generated only by basic research. Applied research, too, can build new knowledge. Nonetheless, basic research is essential for nourishing the expansion of knowledge. Researchers at the center of the scientific community conduct most of the basic research.

b.   Applied Research

Applied researchers try to solve specific policy problems or help practitioners accomplish tasks. The theory is less central to them than seeking a solution to a specific problem for a limited setting. Applied research is frequently descriptive research, and its main strength is its immediate practical use. Applied research is conducted when a decision must be made about a specific real-life problem. Applied research encompasses those studies undertaken to answer questions about specific problems or to make decisions about a particular course of action or policy. For example, an organization contemplating a paperless office and a networking system for the company's personal computers may conduct research to learn the amount of time its employees spend at personal computers in an average week.

c.   Basic and Applied Research Compared

The procedures and techniques utilized by basic and applied researchers do not differ substantially. Both employ the scientific method to answer the questions at hand. The scientific community is the primary consumer of basic research. The consumers of applied research findings are practitioners such as teachers, counselors, and caseworkers, or decision-makers such as managers, committees, and officials. Often, someone other than the researcher who conducted the study uses the results of applied research. This means that applied researchers have an obligation to translate findings from scientific-technical language into the language of decision-makers or practitioners. The results of applied research are less likely to enter the public domain in publications. Results may be available only to a small number of decision-makers or practitioners, who decide whether or how to put the research results into practice and who may or may not use the results.

Applied and basic researchers adopt different orientations toward research methodology. Basic researchers emphasize high standards and try to conduct near-perfect research. Applied researchers make more trade-offs. They may compromise scientific rigor to get quick, usable results. Compromise is no excuse for sloppy research, however. Applied researchers squeeze research into the constraints of an applied setting and balance rigor against practical needs. Such balancing requires an in-depth knowledge of research and an awareness of the consequences of compromising standards.

d.   Types of Applied Research

Practitioners use several types of applied research. Some of the major ones are:

i) **Action research:** The applied research that treats knowledge as a form of power and abolishes the line between research and social action. Those who are being studied participate in the research process; research incorporates ordinary or popular knowledge; research focuses on power with a goal of empowerment; research seeks to raise consciousness or increase awareness, and research is tied directly to political action.

The researchers try to advance a cause or improve conditions by expanding public awareness.

They are explicitly political, not value-neutral. Because the goal is to improve the conditions of research participants, formal reports, articles, or books become secondary. Action researchers assume that knowledge develops from experience, particularly the experience of social-political action. They also assume that ordinary people can become aware of conditions and learn to take actions that can bring about improvement.

ii) **Impact Assessment Research:** Its purpose is to estimate the likely consequences of a planned change. Such an assessment is used for planning and making choices among alternative policies – to make an impact assessment of Basha Dam on the environment; to determine changes in housing if a major new highway is built.

iii) **Evaluation Research:** It addresses the question, "Did it work?" The process of establishing value judgment based on evidence about the achievement of the goals of a program. Evaluation research measures the effectiveness of a program, policy, or way of doing something. "Did the program work?" "Did it achieve its objectives?" Evaluation researchers use several research techniques (survey, field research). Practitioners involved with a policy or program may conduct evaluation research for their own information or at the request of outside decision-makers, who sometimes place limits on researchers by setting boundaries on what can be studied and determining the outcome of interest.

Two types of evaluation research are formative and summative. *Formative evaluation* is built-in monitoring or continuous feedback on a program used for program management. *The summative evaluation* looks at the final program outcomes. Both are usually necessary.

3. Types According to Time Dimension in Research

Another dimension of research is the treatment of time. Some studies give us a snapshot of a single, fixed time point and allow us to analyze it in detail. Other studies provide a moving picture that lets us follow events, people, or sale of products over a period of time. In this way from the angle of time research could be divided into two broad types:

a. Cross-Sectional Research. In *cross-sectional research,* researchers observe at one point in time. Cross-sectional research is usually the simplest and least costly alternative. Its disadvantage is that it cannot capture the change processes. Cross-sectional research can be exploratory, descriptive, or explanatory, but it is most consistent with a descriptive approach to research.

b. Longitudinal Research. Researchers using longitudinal research examine features of people or other units at more than one time. It is usually more complex and costly than cross-sectional research but it is also more powerful, especially when researchers seek answers to questions about change. There are three types of longitudinal research: time series, panel, and cohort.

i.   Time series research is a longitudinal study in which the same type of information is collected on a group of people or other units across multiple time periods. The researcher can observe stability or change in the features of the units or can track conditions over time. One could track the characteristics of students registering in the course on Research Methods over a period of four years i.e. the characteristics (Total, age characteristics, gender distribution, subject distribution, and geographic distribution). Such an analysis could tell us the trends in the character over the four years.

ii.   The panel study is a powerful type of longitudinal research. In a panel study, the researcher observes exactly the same people, group, or organization across time periods. It is difficult to carry out such a study. Tracking people over time is often difficult because some people die or cannot be located. Nevertheless, the results of a well-designed panel study are very valuable.

iii. **A cohort analysis** is similar to the panel study, but rather than observing the exact same people, a category of people who share a similar life experience in a specified time period is studied. The focus is on the cohort, or category, not on specific individuals. Commonly used cohorts include all people born in the same year (called birth cohorts), all people hired at the same time, all people retire on one or two-year time frame and all people who graduate in a given year. Unlike panel studies, researchers do not have to locate the exact same people for cohort studies. The only need to identify those who experienced a common life event.

4. Types According to the Research (data collection) Techniques

Every researcher collects data using one or more techniques. The techniques may be grouped into two categories: *quantitative*, collecting data in the form of numbers, and *qualitative*, collecting data in the form of words or pictures.

a.   Quantitative
The main quantitative techniques are:

1.   Experiments
2.   Surveys
3.   Content Analysis
4.   Using Existing Statistics

b.   Qualitative
The major qualitative techniques of research are:

1.   Field Research
2.   Case Study
3.   Focus Group Discussion.

FRAME OF THE THESIS/ DISSERTATION

- **PRELIMINARY PAGES:** (title page, certificates, abstract, dedication, preface, contents list, etc.)
- **CHAPTERIZATION:** there are five chapters/parts in a thesis/dissertation/research article

1. INTRODUCTION

a. background of the research
b. Introduction to the variables
c. Introduction to the title
d. Introduction to the text or topic
e. Introduction to the selected author for the study
f. Introduction to the theory and model
g. Research gap
h. Research statement/contention/thesis statement
i. Research objectives
j. Research questions
k. Significance of the study
l. The rationale of the study
m. Conclusion of the chapter
n. A brief view of the next chapter

2. LITERATURE REVIEW

a. Introduction the review process (ascending/descending, General to particular/particular to general, thematic or chronological)
b. Review of the papers/thesis related to the model
c. Review of the papers/thesis related to the topic or text
d. Research gap

e.   Conclusion

f.   Brief view about the next chapter

3.   RESEARCH METHODOLOGY

a.   Introduction to the chapter

b.   Introduction of the taken approach (qualitative or quantitative)

c.   Research tools

d.   Sampling

e.   Research design

f.   Formatting style (APA/MLA etc.)

g.   Data analysis method/procedure

h.   Conclusion

i.   A brief view of the next chapter

4.   DATA ANALYSIS

a.   Introduction to the chapter

b.   Introduction of the method or procedure of analysis

c.   Data analysis technique or steps

d.   Data analysis (application)/ process

e.   Conclusion

f.   A brief view of the next chapter

5.   CONCLUSION

a.   A brief view of the researched article/thesis/topic

b.   Review of objectives

c.   Review of questions

d.   Findings of the study

e.   Suggestions for upcoming researchers

f.   Recommendations

g.   Conclusion the chapter

•   ***References/Bibliography***

•   ***Appendix*** (copy of the text, questionnaires, inscribed interview, proofs of data analysis, etc.)

TOPIC
06

DIFFERENCE BETWEEN QUALITATIVE AND QUANTITATIVE RESEARCH

There exists a fundamental distinction between two types of data:

Quantitative Data

Quantitative data is information about quantities, and therefore numbers and qualitative data are descriptive and regards phenomenon which can be observed but not measured, such as language.

Qualitative Research

Qualitative research is empirical research where the data are not in the form of numbers (Punch, 1998, p. 4).

Qualitative research is multimethod in focus, involving an interpretive, naturalistic approach to its subject matter. This means that qualitative researchers study things in their natural settings, attempting to make sense of, or interpret, phenomena in terms of the meanings people bring to them. (Denzin and Lincoln (1994, p. 2)

Methods (used to obtain qualitative data)

Qualitative researchers use a variety of methods to develop deep understandings of how people perceive their social realities and in consequence, how they act within the social world.

For example, diary accounts, open-ended questionnaires, documents, participant observation, and ethnography.

The researcher has several methods for collecting empirical materials, ranging from the interview to direct observation, to the analysis of artifacts, documents, and cultural records, to the use of visual materials or personal experience. (Denzin and Lincoln (1994, p. 14)

A good example of a qualitative research method

would be **unstructured interviews** that generate qualitative data through the use of open questions. This allows the respondent to talk in some depth, choosing their own words. This helps the researcher develop a real sense of a person's understanding of a situation.

Notice that qualitative data could be much more than just words or text. Photographs, videos, sound recordings and so on, can be considered qualitative data.

Data Analysis

Qualitative research is endlessly creative and interpretive. The researcher does not just leave the field with mountains of empirical data and then easily write up his or her findings.

Qualitative interpretations are constructed, and various techniques can be used to make sense of the data, such as **content analysis, grounded theory** (Glaser & Strauss, 1967), **thematic analysis** (Braun & Clarke, 2006) or discourse analysis.

Key Features

Events can be understood adequately only if they are seen in context. Therefore, a qualitative researcher immerses her/himself in the field, in natural surroundings. The contexts of inquiry are not contrived; they are natural. Nothing is predefined or taken for granted.

Qualitative researchers want those who are studied to speak for themselves, to provide their perspectives in words and other actions. Therefore, qualitative research is an interactive process in which the persons studied teach the researcher about their lives.

The qualitative researcher is an integral part of the data, without the active participation of the researcher, no data exists.

The design of the study evolves during the research and can be adjusted or changed as it progresses.

For the qualitative researcher, there is no single reality, it is subjective and exists only in reference to the observer.

The theory is data-driven, and emerges as part of the

research process, evolving from the data as they are collected.

Limitations

Because of the time and costs involved, qualitative designs do not generally draw samples from large-scale data sets.

The problem of adequate validity or reliability is a major criticism. Because of the subjective nature of qualitative data and its origin in single contexts, it is difficult to apply conventional standards of reliability and validity.

For example, because of the central role played by the researcher in the generation of data, it is not possible to replicate qualitative studies. Also, contexts, situations, events, conditions, and interactions cannot be replicated to any extent nor can generalizations be made to a wider context than the one studied with any confidence

The time required for data collection, analysis and interpretation are lengthy. Analysis of qualitative data is difficult and expert knowledge of an area is necessary to try to interpret qualitative data, and great care must be taken when doing so, for example, if looking for symptoms of mental illness.

Strengths

Because of close researcher involvement, the researcher gains an insider's view of the field. This allows the researcher to find issues that are often missed (such as subtleties and complexities) by the scientific, more positivistic inquiries.

Qualitative descriptions can play an important role in suggesting possible relationships, causes, effects, and dynamic processes.

Qualitative analysis allows for ambiguities/ contradictions in the data, which are a reflection of social reality (Denscombe, 2010).

Qualitative research uses a descriptive, narrative style; this research might be of particular benefit to the practitioner as she or he could turn to qualitative reports in order to examine forms of knowledge that might otherwise be unavailable, thereby gaining new insight.

Quantitative Research

Quantitative research gathers data in a numerical form that can be put into categories, or in rank order, or measured in units of measurement. This type of data can be used to construct graphs and tables of raw data.

Quantitative researchers aim to establish general laws of behavior and phenomenon across different settings/contexts. Research is used to test a theory and ultimately support or reject it.

Methods (used to obtain quantitative data)

Experiments typically yield quantitative data, as they are concerned with measuring things. However, other research methods, such as controlled observations and questionnaires can produce both quantitative information.

For example, a rating scale or closed questions on a questionnaire would generate quantitative data as these produce either numerical data or data that can be put into categories (e.g., "yes," "no" answers).

Experimental methods limit the possible ways in which a research participant can react to and express appropriate social behavior.

Findings are therefore likely to be context-bound and simply a reflection of the assumptions which the researcher brings to the investigation.

Data Analysis

Statistics help us turn quantitative data into useful information to help with decision making. We can use statistics to summarize our data, describing patterns, relationships, and connections. Statistics can be descriptive or inferential.

Descriptive statistics help us to summarize our data whereas inferential statistics are used to identify statistically significant differences between groups of data (such as intervention and control groups in a randomized control study).

Key Features

Quantitative researchers try to control extraneous variables by conducting their studies in the lab.

The research aims for objectivity (i.e., without bias),

and is separated from the data.

The design of the study is determined before it begins.

For the quantitative researcher reality is objective and exists separately to the researcher, and is capable of being seen by anyone.

Research is used to test a theory and ultimately support or reject it.

Limitations

Context: Quantitative experiments do not take place in natural settings. In addition, they do not allow participants to explain their choices or the meaning of the questions may have for those participants (Carr, 1994).

Researcher expertise: Poor knowledge of the application of the statistical analysis may negatively affect analysis and subsequent interpretation (Black, 1999).

Variability of data quantity: Large sample sizes are needed for more accurate analysis. Small scale quantitative studies may be less reliable because of the low quantity of data (Denscombe, 2010). This also affects the ability to generalize study findings to wider populations.

Confirmation bias: The researcher might miss observing phenomena because of focus on theory or hypothesis testing rather than on the theory of hypothesis generation.

Strengths

Scientific objectivity: Quantitative data can be interpreted with statistical analysis, and since statistics are based on the principles of mathematics, the quantitative approach is viewed as scientifically objective, and rational (Carr, 1994; Denscombe, 2010).

Useful for testing and validating already constructed theories.

Rapid analysis: Sophisticated software removes much of the need for prolonged data analysis, especially with large volumes of data involved (Antonius, 2003).

Replication: Quantitative data is based on measured values and can be checked by others because numerical data is less open to ambiguities of interpretation.

Hypotheses can also be tested because of the use of statistical analysis (Antonius, 2003).

TOPIC
07

CASE STUDY METHOD

What is a case study research method?

Case studies are in-depth investigations of a single person, topic, issue, problem, text, group, event or community. Typically, data are gathered from a variety of sources and by using several different methods (e.g. observations & interviews).

The case study research method originated in clinical medicine (the case history, i.e. the patient's personal history). In psychology, case studies are often confined to the study of a particular individual.

The information is mainly biographical and relates to events in the individual's past (i.e. retrospective), as well as to significant events that are currently occurring in his or her everyday life.

The case study is not itself a research method, but researchers select methods of data collection and analysis that will generate material suitable for case studies.

Example: Freud (1909a, 1909b) conducted very detailed investigations into the private lives of his patients in an attempt to both understand and help them overcome their illnesses. Even today case histories are one of the main methods of investigation in abnormal psychology and psychiatry.

This makes it clear that the case study is a method that should only be used by a psychologist, therapist or psychiatrist, i.e. someone with a professional qualification.

There is an ethical issue of competence. Only someone qualified to diagnose and treat a person can conduct a formal case study relating to atypical (i.e. abnormal) behavior or atypical development.

How is a case study conducted?

The procedure used in a case study means that the

researcher provides a description of the behavior. This comes from interviews and other sources, such as observation.

The client also reports detail of events from his or her point of view. The researcher then writes up the information from both sources above as the case study and interprets the information.

The research may also continue for an extended period of time, so processes and developments can be studied as they happen.

Amongst the sources of data the psychologist is likely to turn to when carrying out a case study are observations of a person's daily routine, unstructured interviews with the participant herself (and with people who know her), diaries, personal notes (e.g. letters, photographs, notes) or official document (e.g. case notes, clinical notes, appraisal reports).

The case study method often involves simply observing what happens to, or reconstructing 'the case history' of a single participant or group of individuals (such as a school class or a specific social group), i.e. the idiographic approach.

The interview is also an extremely effective procedure for obtaining information about an individual, and it may be used to collect comments from the person's friends, parents, employer, workmates and others who have a good knowledge of the person, as well as to obtain facts from the person him or herself.

Most of this information is likely to be qualitative (i.e. verbal description rather than measurement) but the psychologist might collect numerical data as well.

How to analyze case study data

The data collected can be analyzed using different theories (e.g. grounded theory, interpretative phenomenological analysis, text interpretation, e.g. thematic coding).

All the approaches mentioned here use preconceived categories in the analysis and they are ideographic in their approach, i.e. they focus on the individual case without reference to a comparison group.

Interpreting the information means the researcher

decides what to include or leave out. A good case study should always make clear which information is the factual description and which is an inference or the opinion of the researcher.

Strengths of Case Studies

- Provides detailed (rich qualitative) information.
- Provides insight for further research.
- Permitting investigation of otherwise impractical (or unethical) situations.
- Case studies allow a researcher to investigate a topic in far more detail than might be possible if they were trying to deal with a large number of research participants (nomothetic approach) with the aim of 'averaging'.
- Because of their in-depth, multi-sided approach case studies often shed light on aspects of human thinking and behavior that would be unethical or impractical to study in other ways.
- Research which only looks into the measurable aspects of human behavior is not likely to give us insights into the subjective dimension to experience which is so important to psychoanalytic and humanistic psychologists.
- Case studies are often used in exploratory research. They can help us generate new ideas (that might be tested by other methods). They are an important way of illustrating theories and can help show how different aspects of a person's life are related to each other.

Limitations of Case Studies

- Can't generalize the results to the wider population.
- Researchers' own subjective feeling may influence the case study (researcher bias).
- Difficult to replicate.
- Time-consuming.
- Because a case study deals with only one person/event/group we can never be sure whether the conclusions drawn from this particular case apply elsewhere.
- The results of the study are not generalizable because

we can never know whether the case we have investigated is representative of the wider body of "similar" instances

- Because they are based on the analysis of qualitative (i.e. descriptive) data a lot depends on the interpretation the psychologist places on the information she has acquired.

- This means that there is a lot of scope for observer bias and it could be that the subjective opinions of the psychologist intrude in the assessment of what the data means.

- For example, Freud has been criticized for producing case studies in which the information was sometimes distorted to fit the particular theories about behavior (e.g. Little Hans).

CONCEPTS, PROPOSITION, AND THEORY

The purpose of science concerns the expansion of knowledge, the discovery of truth and to make predictions. Theory building is the means by which the basic researchers hope to achieve this purpose.

A scientist poses questions like: What produces inflation? Does student-teacher interaction influence students' performance? In both these questions, there is the element of prediction i.e. that if we do such and such, then so and so will happen. In fact, we are looking for an explanation for the issue that has been raised in these questions. Underlying the explanation is the whole process through which the phenomenon emerges, and we would like to understand the process to reach prediction.

Prediction and understanding are the two purposes of theory. Accomplishing the first goal allows the theorist to predict the behavior or characteristics of one phenomenon from the knowledge of another phenomenon's characteristics. A business researcher may theorize that older investors tend to be more interested in investment income than younger investors. This theory, once verified, should allow researchers to predict the importance of expected dividend yield on the basis of investors' age. The researcher would also like to understand the process. In most situations prediction and understanding the process go hand in hand i.e. to predict the phenomenon, we must have an explanation of why variables behave as they do. Theories provide these explanations.

Theory

As such theory is a systematic and general attempt to explain something like: Why do people commit crimes? How do the media affect us? Why do some people believe in

God? Why do people get married? Why do kids play truant from school? How is our identity shaped by culture? Each of these questions contains a reference to some observed phenomenon. A suggested explanation for the observed phenomenon is theory. More formally, a **theory** is a coherent set of general propositions, used as principles of explanations of the apparent relationship of certain observed phenomena. A key element in this definition is the term proposition.

- **"Theory"**
- A systematic and general attempt to explain something... A suggested explanation for something...
- "Why do people commit crimes?"
- "How does the media affect us?"
- "Why do some people believe in God?"
- "Why do people get married?"
- "How is our identity shaped by culture?"

Concepts

Theory development is essentially a process of describing phenomena at increasingly higher levels of abstraction. A **concept** (or construct) is a generalized idea about a class of objects, attributes, occurrences, or processes that have been given a name. Such names are created or developed or constructed for the identification of the phenomenon, be it physical or non-physical. All these may be considered as empirical realities e.g. leadership, productivity, morale, motivation, inflation, happiness, banana.

Concepts are the building block of theory. Concepts abstract reality. That is, concepts are expressed in words, letters, signs, and symbols that refer to various events or objects. For example, the concept "asset" is an abstract term that may, in the concrete world of reality, refer to a specific punch press machine. Concepts, however, may vary in degree of abstraction and we can put them in a ladder of abstraction, indicating different levels.

A Ladder of Abstraction for Concepts

- Increasingly more abstract
- Vegetation

- Fruit
- Banana
- Reality

Moving up the **ladder of abstraction,** the basic concept becomes more abstract, wider in scope, and less amenable to measurement. The scientific researcher operates at two levels: on the abstract level of concepts (and propositions) and on the empirical level of variables (and hypotheses). At the empirical level we "experience" reality – that is we observe the objects or events. In this example, the reality has been given a name i.e. banana. Moving up the ladder this reality falls in wider reality i.e. fruit, which in turn becomes part of further wider reality called vegetation.

Researchers are concerned with the observable world, or what we may call as "reality." We try to construct names to such empirical reality for its identification, which may be referred to as concept at an abstract level.

Concepts

OBSERVATION OF OBJECTS AND EVENTS (REALITY)

- Empirical Level
- Abstract Level

Concepts are Abstractions of Reality

Theorists translate their conceptualization of reality into abstract ideas. Thus theory deals with abstraction. Things are not the essence of theory; ideas are. Concepts in isolation are not theories.

Only when we explain how concepts relate to other concepts we begin to construct theories.

Propositions

Concepts are the basic units of theory development. However, theories require an understanding of the relationship among concepts. Thus, once the reality is abstracted into concepts, the scientist is interested in the relationship among various concepts. **Propositions** are statements concerned with the logical relationships among concepts. A proposition explains the logical linkage among certain concepts by asserting a universal connection between concepts.

The theory is an abstraction from observed reality. Concepts are at one level of abstraction. Investigating propositions requires that we increase our level of abstract thinking. When we think about theories, we are at the highest level of abstraction because we are investigating the relationship between propositions.

- *The theory is a network of propositions.*
- Theory Building Is a Process of Increasing Abstraction
- Theories
- Propositions
- Concepts
- Observation of objects and events (reality)
- Increasingly more abstract

CONCEPTS

Things we observe are the observable realities, which could be physical or abstract. For purposes of identification of reality, we try to give a name to it. By using the name we communicate with others and over time it becomes part of our language.

A concept is a generalized idea about a class of objects, attributes, occurrences, or processes that have been given a name. In other words, a concept is an idea expressed as a symbol or in words. Natural science concepts are often expressed in symbolic forms. Most social science concepts are expressed as words. Words, after all, are symbols too; they are symbols we learn with language. Height is a concept with which all of you are familiar. In a sense, a language is merely an agreement to represent ideas by sound or written characters that people learned at some point in their lives. Learning concepts and theory is like learning a language.

Concepts are an Abstraction of Reality

Concepts are everywhere, and you use them all the time. Height is a simple concept form everyday experience. What does it mean? It is easy to use the concept of height, but describing the concept itself is difficult. It represents an abstract idea about physical reality or **an abstraction of reality**. Height is a characteristic of physical objects, the distance from top to bottom. All people, buildings, trees, mountains, books and so forth have height. The word height refers to an abstract idea. We associate its sound and its written form with that idea. There is nothing inherent in the sounds that make up the word and the idea it represents. The connection is arbitrary, but it is still useful. People can express the abstract idea to one another using symbols.

In other words, concepts are the abstractions of reality physical of non-physical like a table, leadership, productivity, and morale are all labels given to some phenomenon (reality). The concepts stand for the phenomenon, not the phenomenon itself; hence it may be called **an abstraction of empirical reality**.

Degree of Abstraction

Concepts vary in their level of abstraction. They are on a continuum from the most concrete to the most abstract. Very concrete ones refer to straightforward physical objects or familiar experiences (e.g. height, school, age, family income, or housing). More abstract concepts refer to ideas that have a diffuse, indirect expression (e.g. family dissolution, racism, political power)

The organization of concepts in sequence from the most concrete and individual to the most general indicates the degree of abstraction.

Moving up the ladder of abstraction, the basic concept becomes more abstract, wider in scope, and less amenable to measurement. The scientific researcher operates at two levels of concepts (and propositions) and on the empirical level of variables. At the empirical level we experience reality – that is we observe objects or events.

Sources of Concepts

Everyday culture is filled with concepts, but many of them have vague and unclear definitions. Likewise, the values and experiences of people in culture may limit everyday concepts. Nevertheless, we borrow concepts from everyday culture; though these to be refined.

We create concepts from personal experiences, creative thought, or observation. The classical theorist originated many concepts like family system, gender role, socialization, self-worth, frustration, and displaced aggression.

We also borrow concepts from sister disciplines.

Importance of Concepts

Concepts form a specialized language or *jargon*. Specialists use jargon as a shorthand way to communicate with one another. Most fields have their own jargon. Physicians, lawyers, engineers, accountants, plumbers, and auto mechanics all have specialized languages. They use their jargon to refer to the ideas and objects with which they work. Special problems grow out of the need for concept precision and inventiveness. Vague meanings attached to a concept create problems of measurement. Therefore, not only the construction of concepts is necessary but also these should be precise and the researchers should have some agreement to its meaning. Identification of concepts is necessary because we use concepts in hypothesis formulation. Here too one of the characteristics of a good hypothesis is that it should be conceptually clear. The success of research hinges on

(1)   How clearly we conceptualize and

(2)   How well others understand the concept we use.

For example, we might ask respondents for an estimate of their family income. This may seem to be a simple, unambiguous concept, but we may receive varying and confusing answers unless we restrict or narrow the concept by specifying:

- Time period, such as weekly, monthly, or annually.
- Before or after income taxes.
- For the head of the family only or for all family members.
- For salary and wages only or also for dividends, interest, and capital gains.
- Income in kinds, such as free rent, employee discounts, or food stamps.

Definitions

Confusion about the meaning of concepts can destroy a research study's value without the researcher even knowing it. If words have different meanings to the different groups involved, then they are not communicating on the same wave-length. Definitions are one way to reduce this danger.

Dictionary Definitions

Researchers must struggle with two types of definitions. In the more familiar dictionary, a concept is defined with synonyms. For example, a customer is defined as a patron: a patron, in turn, is defined as a customer or client of an establishment; a client is defined as one who employs the services of any professional ..., also loosely, a patron of any shop. These circular definitions may be adequate for general communication but not for research.

Dictionary definitions are also called conceptual or theoretical or nominal definitions. The conceptual definition is a definition in abstract, theoretical terms. It refers to other ideas or constructs. There is no magical way to turn a construct into a precise conceptual definition. It involves thinking carefully, observing directly, consulting with others, reading what others have said, and trying possible definitions.

A single construct can have several definitions, and people may disagree over definitions. Conceptual definitions are linked to theoretical frameworks and to value positions. For example, a conflict theorist may define *social class* as the power and property of a group of people in a society has or lacks. A structural functionalist defines it in terms of individuals who share a social status, lifestyle, or subjective justification. Although people disagree over definitions, the researcher should always state explicitly which definition he or she is using.

Some constructs are highly abstract and complex. They contain lower-level concepts within them (e.g. powerlessness), which can be made even more specific (e.g. a feeling of little power over wherever on lives). Other concepts are concrete and simple (e.g. age). When developing definitions, a researcher needs to be aware of how complex and abstract a construct is. For example, a concrete construction such as age is easier to define (e.g. the number of years that have passed since birth) which is a complex, abstract concept such as morale.

Operational Definition

In research, we must measure concepts and constructs, and this requires more rigorous definitions. A concept must be made operational in order to be measured. An operational definition gives meaning to a concept by specifying the activities or operations necessary to measure it. An operational definition specifies what must be done to measure the concept under investigation. It is like a manual of instruction or a recipe: do such-and-such in so-and-so manner.

An operational definition is also called a *working definition* stated in terms of specific testing or measurement criteria. The concepts must have empirical referents (i.e. we must be able to count, measure, or in some other way gather the information through our senses). Whether the object to be defined is physical e.g. a machine tool) or highly abstract (e.g. achievement motivation), the definition must specify characteristics and how to be observed. The specification and procedures must be so clear that any competent person using them would classify the objects the same way. So in the operational definition, we must specify concrete indicators that can be observed/measured (observable indicators).

Use both Definitions in Research

Look at the observable phenomenon, we construct a label for it, then try to define it theoretically, which gives a lead to the development of criteria for its measurement, and finally, we gather the data

TOPIC
10

VARIABLES AND TYPES OF VARIABLES

Variable is a central idea in research. Simply defined, the variable is a concept that varies.

There are two types of concepts: those that refer to a fixed phenomenon and those that vary in quantity, intensity, or amount. The second type of concept and measures of the concept are variables.

A variable is defined as anything that varies or changes in value.

Variables take on two or more values. Because variable represents a quality that can exhibit differences in value, usually magnitude or strength, it may be said that a variable generally is anything that may assume different numerical or categorical values. Once you begin to look for them, you will see variables everywhere.

For example, gender is a variable; it can take two values: male or female. Marital status is a variable; it can take on values of never married, single, married, divorced, or widowed. Family income is a variable; it can take on values from zero to billions of Rupees. A person's attitude toward women empowerment is variable; it can range from highly favorable to highly unfavorable. In this way the variation can be in quantity, intensity, amount, or type; the examples can be production units, absenteeism, gender, religion, motivation, grade, and age. A variable may be situation-specific; for example, gender is a variable but if in a particular situation like a class of Research Methods if there are only female students, then in this situation gender will not be considered as a variable.

Types of Variable

1. Continuous and Discontinuous variables

Variables have different properties and to these properties, we assign numerical values. If the values of a variable can be divided into fractions then we call it a *continuous variable*. Such a variable can take an infinite number of values. Income, temperature, age, or test scores are examples of continuous variables. These variables may take on values within a given range or, in some cases, an infinite set.

Any variable that has a limited number of distinct values and which cannot be divided into fractions is a *discontinuous variable*. Such a variable is also called a *categorical variable* or *classificatory variable*, or *discrete variable*. Some variables have only two values, reflecting the presence or absence of a property: employed-unemployed or male-female have two values. These variables are referred to as dichotomous. There are others that can take added categories such as the demographic variables of race, religion. All such variables that produce data that fit into categories are said to be discrete/categorical/classificatory since only certain values are possible. An automotive variable, for example, where "Chevrolet" is assigned a 5 and "Honda" is assigned a 6, provides no option for a 5.5 (i.e. the values cannot be divided into fractions).

2. Dependent and Independent Variables

Researchers who focus on causal relations usually begin with an effect, and then search for its causes.

The cause variable, or the one that identifies forces or conditions that act on something else, is the *independent variable*. The variable that is the effect or is the result or outcome of another variable is the *dependent variable* (also referred to as outcome variable or effect variable). The independent variable is "independent of" prior causes that act on it, whereas the dependent variable "depends on" the cause.

It is not always easy to determine whether a variable is independent or dependent. Two questions help to identify the independent variable. First, does it come before other variables in time? Second, if the variables occur at the same time, does the researcher suggest that one variable has an impact on another variable? Independent variables affect or have an impact on other variables. When the independent variable is present, the dependent variable is also present, and with each unit of increase in the independent variable, there is an increase or decrease in the dependent variable also. In other words, the variance independent variable is accounted for by the independent variable. The dependent variable is also referred to as the *criterion* variable.

In statistical analysis, a variable is identified by the symbol (X) for the independent variable and by the symbol (Y) for the dependent variable. In the research vocabulary, different labels have been associated with the independent and dependent variables like:

Independent variable	Dependent variable
Presumed cause	*presumed effect*
Stimulus	*Response*
Predicted from	*Predicted to ...*
Antecedent	*Consequence*
Manipulated	*Measured outcome*

Predictor Criterion.

Research studies indicate that successful new product development has an influence on the stock market price of a company. That is, the more successful the new product turns out to be, the higher will be the stock market price of that firm. Therefore, the **success of the new product** is the *independent variable*, and the **stock market price** the *dependent variable*.

The degree of the perceived success of the new product developed will explain the variance in the stock market price of the company.

It is important to remember that there are no preordained variables waiting to be discovered "out there" that are automatically assigned to be independent or dependent. It is, in fact, the product of the researcher's imagination demonstrated convincingly.

3. Moderating Variables

A moderating variable is one that has a strong *contingent* effect on the independent variable-dependent variable relationship. That is, the presence of a third variable (the moderating variable) modifies the original relationship between the independent and the dependent variable.

For example, a strong relationship has been observed between the quality of library facilities (X) and the performance of the students (Y). Although this relationship is supposed to be true generally, it is nevertheless contingent on the interest and inclination of the students. It means that only those students who have the interest and inclination to use the library will show improved performance in their studies.

In this relationship **interest and inclination** is moderating variable i.e. which moderates the strength of the association between X and Y variables.

4. Intervening Variables

A basic causal relationship requires only the independent and dependent variables. The third type of variable, the *intervening variable,* appears in more complex causal relationships. It comes between the independent and dependent variables and shows the link or mechanism between them. Advances in knowledge depend not only on documenting cause and effect relationship but also on specifying the mechanisms that account for the causal relation. In a sense, the intervening variable acts as a dependent variable with respect to the independent variable and acts as an independent variable toward the dependent variable.

A theory of suicide states that married people are less likely to commit suicide than single people. The assumption is that married people have greater social integration (e.g. feelings of belonging to a group or family). Hence a major cause of one type of suicide was that people lacked a sense of belonging to a group (family). Thus this theory can be restated as a three-variable relationship: marital status (independent variable) causes the degree of social integration (intervening variable), which affects suicide (dependent variable). Specifying the chain of causality makes the linkages in theory clearer and helps a researcher test complex relationships.

Look at another finding that a five-day workweek results in higher productivity. What is the process of moving from the independent variable to the dependent variable? What exactly is that factor which theoretically affects the observed phenomenon but cannot be seen? Its effects must be inferred from the effects of an independent variable on the dependent variable. In this work-week hypothesis, one might view the intervening variable to be job satisfaction. To rephrase the statement it could be: the introduction of the five-day workweek (IV) will increase job satisfaction (IVV), which will lead to higher productivity (DV).

5.   Extraneous Variables

An almost infinite number of extraneous variables (EV) exist that might conceivably affect a given relationship. Some can be treated as independent or moderating variables, but most must either be assumed or excluded from the study. Such variables have to be identified by the researcher. In order to identify the true relationship between the independent and the dependent variable, the effect of the extraneous variables may have to be controlled. This is necessary if we are conducting an experiment where the effect of the confounding factors has to be controlled. Confounding factors is another name used for extraneous variables.

Relationship among Variables

Once the variables relevant to the topic of research have been identified, then the researcher is interested in the relationship among them. A statement containing the variable is called a proposition. It may contain one or more than one variable. The proposition having one variable in it may be called a univariate proposition, those with two variables as a bivariate proposition, and then of course multivariate containing three or more variables. Prior to the formulation of a proposition the researcher has to develop strong logical arguments that could help in establishing the relationship. For example, age at marriage and education are the two variables that could lead to a proposition: the higher the education, the higher the age at marriage. What could be the logic to reach this conclusion? All relationships have to be explained with strong logical arguments. If the relationship refers to observable reality, then the proposition can be put to test, and any testable proposition is a hypothesis.

———————

REVIEW OF LITERATURE

A literature review is based on the assumption that knowledge accumulates and that we learn from and build on what others have done. Scientific research is a collective effort of many researchers who share their results with one another and who pursue knowledge as a community. Today's studies build on those of yesterday. Researchers read studies to compare, replicate, or criticize them for weaknesses.

Goals of a Literature Review

Reviews vary in scope and depth. Different kinds of reviews are stronger at fulfilling the different goals of the review. The goals of the review are:

1.   To demonstrate a familiarity with a body of knowledge and establish credibility. A review tells the reader that the researcher knows the research in an area and knows the major issues. A good review increases a reader's confidence in the researcher's professional competence, ability, and background.

2.   To know the path of prior research and how a current research project *is linked to it.* A review outlines the direction, ability, and background of research on a question and shows the development of knowledge. A good review places a research project in a context and demonstrates its relevance by making connections to a body of knowledge.

3.   To integrate and summarize what is known in an area. A review pulls together and synthesizes different results. A good review points out areas where prior studies agree, where they disagree, and where major questions remain. It collects what is known to a point in time and indicates the direction for future research. No reinventing the wheel. No wastage of effort.

4. **To learn from others and stimulate new ideas.** A review tells what others have found so that a researcher can benefit from the efforts of others. A good review identifies blind alleys and suggests hypotheses for replication. It divulges procedures, techniques, and research designs worth copying so that a researcher can better focus hypotheses and gain new insights.

5. **Identification of variables.** Important variables that are likely to influence the problem situation are not left out of the study.

6. **It helps in developing a theoretical framework.**

Types of Reviews

When beginning a review, the researcher may decide on a topic or field of knowledge to examine, how much depth to go into, and the kind of review to conduct. There are six types of review:

1. *Self-study reviews increase the reader's confidence.* A review that only demonstrates familiarity with an area is rarely published but it often is part of an educational program. In addition to giving others confidence in a reviewer's command of the field, it has the side benefit of building the reviewer's self-confidence.

2. *Context reviews place a specific project in the big picture.* One of the goals of review is creating a link to a developing body of knowledge. This is a background or context review. It introduces the rest of the research and establishes the significance and relevance of a research question. It tells the reader how a project fits into the big picture and its implications for a field of knowledge. The review can summarize how the current research continues a developing line of thought, or it can point to a question or unresolved conflict in prior research to be addressed.

3. *Historical review traces the development of an issue over time.* It traces the development of an idea or shows how a particular issue or theory has evolved over time. Researchers conduct a historical review only on the most important ideas in a field.

4. *Theoretical reviews compare how different theories address an issue.* It presents different theories that purport to explain the same thing, then evaluates how well each accounts for findings. In addition to examining the consistency of predictions with findings, a theoretical review may compare theories for the soundness of their assumptions, logical consistency, and scope of explanation. Researchers also use it to integrate two theories or extend the theory to new issues. It sometimes forms a hybrid – the historical theoretical review.

5.   ***The integrative review*** *summarizes what is known at a point in time.* It presents the current state of knowledge and pulls together disparate research reports in a fast-growing area of knowledge.

6.   ***Methodological reviews*** *point out how methodology varies by study.* In it, the researcher evaluates the methodological strength of past studies. It describes conflicting results and shows how different research designs, samples, measures, and so, on account for different results.

Where to find the Research Literature

- Computer: online systems.
- Scholarly journals.
- Books – containing reports of original research, or collection of research articles. READERS or Book of Readings.
- Dissertations.
- Government documents.
- Policy reports and presented papers.
- Bibliographic indexes.

TOPIC
12

CONDUCTING A SYSTEMATIC LITERATURE REVIEW

Define and refine a topic

Prior to the review of the literature have a good idea of the topic of your interest. Although the new thoughts emerging out of the review of literature may help in refocusing the topic, still the researcher needs to have some clear research questions that could guide him/her in the pursuit of relevant material.

Therefore begin a literature review with a clearly defined, well-focused research question and a plan. A good review topic should be as focused on a research question. For example "crime" as such may be too broad a topic. A more focus may be a specific "type of crime" or "economic inequality and crime rates." Often a researcher will not finalize a specific research question for a study until he or she has reviewed the literature. The review helps bring greater focus to the research question.

Design a search

The researcher needs to decide on the type of review, its extensiveness and the types of material to include. The key is to be careful, systematic, and organized. Set parameters on your search; how much time you will devote to it, how far back in time you will look, the maximum number of research reports you will examine, how many libraries you will visit, and so forth.

Also, decide how to record the bibliographic citations for each reference. Maybe begin a file folder or computer file in which you can place possible sources and ideas for new sources.

Locate research reports

Locating research reports depends on the type of report or "outlet" of research being searched. Use multiple search strategies in order to counteract the limitations of a single search method.

Articles in Scholarly Journals. Most social and behavioral research is likely published in scholarly journals. These journals are the vehicles of communication in science. There are dozens of journals, many going back decades, each containing many articles. Locating the relevant articles is a formidable task.

Many academic fields have "abstracts" or "indexes" for the scholarly literature. Find them in the reference section of the library. (Many available on computing as well). Such indexes and abstracts are published regularly.

Another resource for locating articles is the computerized literature search. Researchers organize computerized searches in several ways – by author, by article title, by subject, or by keyword. A *keyword* is an important term for a topic that is likely to be found in a title. You will want to use six to eight keywords in most computer-based searches and consider several synonyms.

Scholarly Books. Finding scholarly books on a subject can be difficult. The subject topics of library catalog systems are usually incomplete and too broad to be useful. A person has to be well conversant with the library cataloging system.

Dissertations. A publication called *Dissertation Abstract International* lists most dissertations. It organizes dissertations by broad subject category, author, and date.

Government Documents. The "government documents" sections of libraries contain specialized lists of government documents.

Policy Reports and Presented Papers. The most difficult sources to locate are policy reports and presented papers. They are listed in some bibliographies of published studies; some are listed in the abstracts or indexes.

What to Record

After you locate a source, you should write down all details of the reference (full names of the authors, titles, volumes, issue, pages)

Write the Review

- A literature review requires planning and good, clear writing, which requires a lot of rewriting. Keep your purposes in mind when you write, and communicate clearly and effectively.

- To prepare a good review, read articles and other literature critically. Skepticism is the norm of science.

- It means that you should not accept what is written simply on the basis of the authority of its having been published. Question what you read, and evaluate it.

- Critically reading research reports requires skills and takes time and practice to develop. When reading an article, read carefully to see whether the introduction and title really fit with the rest of the article.

- Sometimes, titles, abstracts, or the introduction are misleading. They may not fully explain the research project's method and results.

The most critical areas of an article to read are the methods and results sections. Few studies are perfect. Researchers do not always describe the methods they used as fully as they should. Sometimes the results presented in tables or charts do not match what the researcher says. Some points may be overemphasized and others ignored. Check the conclusions; these may not be consistent with the results.

What does a good review look like?

The author should communicate a review's purpose to the reader by its organization. The wrong way to write a review is to list a series of research reports with a summary of the findings of each. This fails to communicate a sense of purpose. It reads like a set of notes strung together. Perhaps the reviewer got sloppy and skipped over the important organizing step in writing the review.

The right way to write a review is to organize common findings or arguments together. A well-accepted approach is to address the most important ideas first, to logically link statements or findings, and to note discrepancies or weaknesses in the present.

The writing process

Your audience

Professional writers say: Always know for whom are you writing. This is because communication is more effective when it is tailored to a specific audience. You should write a research report differently depending on whether the primary audience is the instructor, students, professional colleagues, practitioners, or the general public. It goes without saying that the writing should be clear, accurate, and organized. Instructors assign reports for different reasons and may place requirements on how it is written. In general, instructors want to see writing an organization that reflects clear, logical thinking. Student reports should demonstrate a solid grasp of substantive and methodological concepts. A good way to do this is to use technical terms explicitly when appropriate: they should not be used excessively and incorrectly.

Literature Review Process: Practical Steps

1. Take researcher articles, papers, theses (*most recent ones) on your selected text/topic and on your theory/model.

2. Read all related works, and organize them into ascending or descending order

3. First, write Introduction of literature review in which tells about your collected research work and how would you present them (Ascending/descending order, from most important to least important or from least important to most important).

4. Write a review on the works related to the selected model or theory

5. Write a review on the selected works of taken text or topic/issue/problem

6. In closing part of The Review, Announce Research Gap, and tells how your work is important and different than preceding research works.

TOPIC
13

MEASUREMENT OF CONCEPTS

In everyday usage, measurement occurs when an established yardstick verifies the height, weight, or another feature of a physical object. How well you like a song, a painting, or the personality of a friend is also measurement. In a dictionary sense, to measure is to discover the extent, dimensions, quantity, or capacity of something, especially by comparison with a standard. We measure casually in daily life, but in research the requirements for measurement are rigorous. Certain things lend themselves to easy measurement through the use of appropriate instruments, as for example, physiological phenomena pertaining to human beings such as blood pressure, pulse rates, and body temperature, as well as certain physical attributes such as height and weight. But when we get into the realm of people's subjective feelings, attitudes, ideology, deviance, and perceptions, the measurement of these factors or variables becomes difficult. Like the natural scientist who invents indirect measures of the "invisible" objects and forces of the physical world (magnetism – the force that moves a metal toward the magnet), the social researcher devises measures for difficult- to observe aspects of the social world. For example, suppose you heard a principal complain about teacher morale in a school. Teacher morale is an empirical reality, and we can create some instruments for its measurement.

Measurement in Quantitative and Qualitative Research

Both qualitative and quantitative researchers use careful, systematic methods to gather high-quality data.

Yet, differences in the styles of research and the types of data mean they approach the measurement process differently. Designing precise ways to measure variables is a vital step in planning a study for quantitative researchers. Qualitative researchers use a wider variety of techniques to measure and create new measures while collecting data Here we shall focus on quantitative measurement. Here measurement consists of assigning numbers to empirical events in compliance with set rules. This definition implies that measurement is a three-part process:

1.   Selecting observable empirical events.
2.   Developing a set of mapping rules: a scheme for assigning numbers or symbols to represent aspects of the event being measured.
3.   Applying the mapping rule(s) to each observation of that event.

Assume you are studying people who attend an auto show where all year's new models are on display.

You are interested in learning the male-to-female ratio among attendees. You observe those who enter the show area. If a person is female, you record an F; if male, an M. Any other symbols such as 0 and 1 may also be used if you know what group the symbol identifies.

Researchers might also want to measure the desirability of the styling of the new Espace van. They interview a sample of visitors and assign, with a different mapping rule, their opinions to the following scale:

What is your opinion of the styling of the Espace van?

**Very desirable 5_____4_____3_____2_____
1 Very undesirable**

We can assign a weight-age (score) like:

5   if it is very desirable
4   if desirable
3   if neither
2   if undesirable
1   if very undesirable.

All measurement theorists would call such an opinion rating scale as a form of measurement.

Researchers use two processes: conceptualization and operationalization in measurement.

a.   Conceptualization

Conceptualization is the process of taking a construct and refining it by giving it a conceptual or theoretical definition. A conceptual definition is a definition in abstract, theoretical terms. It refers to other ideas or constructs. There is no magical way to turn a construct into a precise conceptual definition. It involves thinking carefully, observing directly, consulting with others, reading what others have said, and trying possible definitions.

b.   Operationalization

Operationalization is the process of linking the conceptual definition to a specific set of measurement techniques or procedures. It links the language of theory with the language of empirical measures.

The theory is full of abstract concepts, assumptions, relationships, definitions, and causality. Empirical measures describe how people concretely measure specific variables. They refer to specific operations or things people use to indicate the presence of a construct that exists in observable reality.

Operationalization is done by looking at the behavioral dimensions, facets, or properties denoted by the concept. These are then translated into observable elements so as to develop an index of measurement of the concept. Operationally defining a concept involves a series of steps.

Here is an example.

Operational definition: Dimensions and Elements An example

Let us try to operationally define **job satisfaction,** a concept of interest to educators, managers, and students alike. What behavioral dimensions or facets or characteristics would we expect to find in people with high job satisfaction? Let us, first of all, have a conceptual definition of job satisfaction. We can start it like this:

- Employees' feelings toward their job.
- Degree of satisfaction that individuals obtain from various roles they play in an organization.
- A pleasurable or positive emotional feeling resulting from the appraisal of one's job or job experience.
- Employee's perception of how well the job provides those things ('something') that are important. These things are the dimensions of job satisfaction.

Dimensions of job satisfaction: For measuring job satisfaction it is appropriate to look at this concept from different angles relating to work. While employed in an organization the workers might be looking for many "things." Each of these things may be considered as a dimension; a person may be highly satisfied on one dimension and maybe least satisfied on the other one. Those things that have usually been considered important at the place of work can be:

- The work itself.
- Pay/fringe benefits.
- Promotion opportunities.
- Supervision.
- Coworkers.
- Working conditions.

On each dimension, the researcher has to develop logical arguments showing how this particular aspect (thing) relating to a worker's job is important whereby it has a bearing on his/her job satisfaction.

Elements of job satisfaction: It means breaking each dimension further into actual patterns of behavior that would be exhibited through the perception of the workers in an organization. Here again, the researcher shall develop a logical rationale for using a particular element for measuring a specific dimension. For example, let us look at each dimension and some of the corresponding elements:

- Work itself: Elements Opportunities to learn, sense of accomplishment, challenging work, routine work.

- Pay/fringe benefits: Elements. Pay according to qualifications, comparison with other organizations, annual increments, and availability of bonuses, old-age benefits, insurance benefits, and other allowances.

- Promotion opportunities: Elements Mobility policy, equitable, dead-end job.

- Supervision: Elements Employee centered on employee participation in decisions.

- Coworkers: Elements Primary group relations, supportive attitude, level of cohesiveness.

- Working conditions: Elements Lighting arrangements, temperature, cleanliness, building security, hygienic conditions, first aid facility, availability of canteen, availability of toilet facilities, availability of a place for prayer.

On each element ask a question (s), make statements. Look into the scalability of questions. The responses can be put on a scale indicating high satisfaction to the least satisfaction. In many cases, the responses are put on a five-point scale (usually called a Likert scale).

Scales and Indexes

Scales and indexes are often used interchangeably. Social researchers do not use a consistent nomenclature to distinguish between the two.

A scale is a measure in which a researcher captures the intensity, direction, level, or potency of a variable construct. It arranges responses or observations on a continuum or in a series of categories. A scale can use a single indicator or multiple indicators.

An index is a measure in which a researcher adds or combines several distinct indicators of a construct into a single score. The composite scores are often a simple sum of the multiple indicators. Indexes are often measured at the interval or ratio level.

Researchers sometimes combine thee features of scales and indexes in a single measure. This is common when a researcher has several indicators that scale (i.e. that measure intensity or direction). The researcher then adds these indicators together to yield a single score, thereby creating an index.

Types of Scales

A scale refers to any series of items that are arranged progressively according to value or magnitude, into which an item can be placed according to its quantification. In other words, a scale is a continuous spectrum or series of categories.

It is traditional to classify scales of measurement on the basis of the mathematical comparisons that are allowable with these scales. Four types of scales are nominal, ordinal, interval, and ratio.

Nominal Scale

A nominal scale is the one in which the numbers or letters assigned to objects serve as labels for identification or classification. This measurement scale is the simplest type. With nominal data, we are collecting information on a variable that naturally or by design can be grouped into two or more categories that are mutually exclusive, and collectively exhaustive.

Nominal scales are the least powerful of the four scales. They suggest no order or distance relationship and have no arithmetic origin. Nevertheless, if no other scale can be used, one can almost always one set of properties into a set of equivalent classes.

Ordinal Scale

Ordinal scales include the characteristics of the nominal scale plus an indicator of order. If *a* is greater than *b* and *b* is greater than *c*, then *a* is greater than *c*. The use of ordinal scale implies a statement of "greater than" or "less than" without stating how much greater or less. Other descriptors can be: "superior to," "happier than," "poorer than," or "above."

Interval Scale

Interval scales have the power of nominal and ordinal scales plus one additional strength: they incorporate the concept of equality of interval (the distance between 1 and 2 equals the distance between 2 and 3). For example, the elapsed time between 3 and 6 A. M. equals the time between 4 and 7 A. M.

One cannot say, however, 6 A.M. is twice as late as 3 A.M. because "zero time" is an arbitrary origin. In the consumer price index, if the base year is 1983, the price level during 1983 will be set arbitrarily as 100. Although this is an equal interval measurement scale, the zero points are arbitrary.

Ratio Scale

Ratio scales incorporate all the powers of the previous scales plus the provision for absolute zero or origin. Ratio data represent the actual amounts of a variable. Measures of physical dimensions such as weight, height, distance, and area are examples. The absolute zero represents a point on the scale where there is an absence of the given attribute. If we hear that a person has zero amount of money, we understand the zero value of the amount.

TOPIC
14

THE RESEARCH PROPOSAL

A research *proposal* is a document that presents a plan for a project to reviewers for evaluation. It can be a supervised project submitted to instructors as part of an educational degree (e.g. a Master's thesis or a Ph.D. dissertation) or it can be a research project proposed to a funding agency. Its purpose is to convince reviewers that the researcher is capable of successfully conducting the proposed research project. Reviewers have more confidence that a planned project will be successfully completed if the proposal is well written and organized, and carefully planned.

The proposal is just like a research report, but it is written before the research project begins. A proposal describes the research problem and its importance and gives a detailed account of the methods that will be used and why they are appropriate.

A proposal for quantitative research has most of the parts of a research report: a title, an abstract, a problem statement, a literature review, a method or design section, and a bibliography. It lacks results, discussion, and conclusions section. The proposal has a plan for data collection and analysis. It frequently includes a schedule of the steps to be undertaken and an estimate of the time required for each step.

For funded projects, the researchers need to show a track record of past success in the proposal, especially if they are going to be in charge of the project. Proposals usually include curriculum vitae, letters of support from other researchers, and record if past research.

Research Proposal Sections

Introduction
- Background of the study
- Objectives
- Significance

Research Design
- Data collection technique (survey, experiment, qualitative technique)
- Population & Sample
- The tool of data collection
- Data Gathering
- Data processing and analysis
- Report writing
- Budget
- Time Schedule
- Team of Researchers

Parts of Research proposal in English Studies (Humanities Research)

1. **Title** (not more than 20 words)
2. **Abstract** (150 words to 250 words)
3. **Introduction** (Background of the study, an intro of the topic, an intro of variables, an intro of the selected text, an intro of the author or area, an intro of theory, an intro of theorist/model)
4. **Literature review** (Review on text, review on the model, research gap)
5. **Significance of the study** (three-dimensional significance; Social Significance, academic significance, personal significance)
6. **Research Questions**
7. **Objectives of the research**
8. **Theoretical framework**
9. **Research methodology**
10. **Data analysis** (Exemplary)
11. **Conclusions** (Tentative)
12. **References**

TOPIC
15

THEORETICAL FRAMEWORK

A **theoretical framework** is a conceptual model of how one theorizes or makes logical sense of the relationships among several factors that have been identified as important to the problem under study.

These factors which may also be called variables may have been identified through such processes as interviews with informants, observations, and literature surveys. The theoretical framework discusses the interrelationships among the variables that are considered to be integral to the dynamics of the situation being investigated. Developing such a conceptual framework helps us to postulate or hypothesize and test certain relationships and thus improve our understanding of the dynamics of the situation. From the theoretical framework, then, testable hypotheses can be developed to examine whether the theory formulated is valid or not. The hypothesized relationships can thereafter be tested through appropriate statistical analysis.

Hence the entire research rests on the basis of the theoretical framework. Even if the testable hypotheses not necessarily generated, developing a good theoretical framework is central to examining the problem under investigation.

There is a relationship between the literature survey and the theoretical framework whereby the former provides a solid foundation for developing the latter. A literature survey helps in the identification of the relevant variables, as determined by the previous researches. This in addition to other logical connections that can be conceptualized forms the basis for the theoretical model. The theoretical framework elaborates on the relationships among the variables, explains the theory underlying these relations, and describes the nature and direction of the relationships. Just as the literature survey sets the stage for a good theoretical framework, this, in turn, provides the logical base for developing useable hypotheses. From the preceding discussion, it can be concluded that a theoretical framework is none other than identifying the network of relationships among the variables considered important to the study of any given problem situation. Therefore, the theoretical framework offers the conceptual foundation for constructing the edifice of research that is to take in hand.

A theoretical framework:

- Elaborates the relationship among the variables.
- Explains the logic underlying these relationships.
- Describes the nature, and direction of the relationships.

In the review of literature, it is possible that you may come across a number of theories readily available for adoption as a theoretical framework for the study under consideration. Theories are supposed to be generic whereby they could be applicable to different situations. Some concepts borrowed from such theories may have to be replaced with arguments, logic explicated, and the framework may be readily available. It is also possible that the researcher may combine more than one existing theory and come up with an entirely new framework, and in the process may develop new concepts as well.

However, in the absence of the readymade conceptual framework, the researcher may venture to develop his/her own framework. Though, the researcher has to depend a lot on the existing body of literature for the identification of variables as well as for developing a rigorous logical argumentation for the interrelationships among different variables.

Whether the researcher uses a ready-made theoretical framework or explicates an entirely new one, there are some essential features that have to be taken into consideration. These features may be called as components of a theoretical framework.

The Components of the Theoretical Framework

A good theoretical framework identifies and labels the important variables in the situation that are relevant to the problem identified. It logically describes the interconnections among these variables.

The relationships among the independent variables, the dependent variable(s), and if applicable, the moderating and intervening variables are elaborated. The elaboration of the variables in the theoretical framework addresses the issues of why or how we expect certain relationships to exist, and the nature and direction of the relationships among the variables of interest.

There are six basic features that should be incorporated in any theoretical framework.

These features are:

1. Make an inventory of variables: For developing a framework it appears essential to identify the factors relevant to the problem under study. These factors are the empirical realities that can be named at some abstract level called concepts. The concepts taking more than one value are the variables. In other words, the researcher makes *an inventory of relevant variables*. The variables considered relevant to the study should be clearly identified and labeled in the discussion.

2. Specify the direction of relationship: If the nature and direction of relationship can be theorized on the basis of the findings of previous research, then there should be an indication in the discussion as to whether the relationship should be positive or negative.

3. Give a clear explanation of why we should expect the proposed relationships to exist: There should be a clear explanation of why we would expect these relationships to exist. The arguments could be drawn from the previous research findings. The discussions should state how two or more variables are related to one another. This should be done for the important relationships that are theorized to exist among the variables. It is essential to theorize the logical relationship between different variables.

4. Make an inventory of propositions: Stipulation of the logical relationship between any two variables means the formulation of a proposition. If such relationships have been proposed between different variables, it will result in the formulation of a number of propositions. Let us call such a collection of propositions as *an inventory of propositions.* Each proposition is backed up by strong theoretical argumentation.

5. Arrange these propositions in sequential order: one proposition generates the next proposition, which generates the next following proposition, which in turn generates the next following proposition, and so on. This is an axiomatic way of the derivation of propositions.

Resultantly it will provide us a sequentially arranged set of propositions that are interlinked and interlocked with each other. Theory, if you remember, is an interrelated set of propositions. Therefore, the present interrelated set of propositions relevant to a particular problem is, in fact, a theoretical framework explaining the pathways of logical relationships between different variables.

6. A schematic diagram of the theoretical model be given: A schematic diagram of the theoretical framework should be given so that the reader can see and easily comprehend the theorized relationships. **Example:**

Research Question: Why middle-class families decline in their size?

By following the guidelines discussed earlier let us develop a theoretical framework.

1. Inventory of variables: Education levels of the couples, age at marriage, working women, rationalism, exposure to mass media of communication, accessibility to health services, practicing of family planning practices, aspirations about the education of children, shift to nuclear families, mobility orientation.

2. Specify the direction of relationship: Higher education higher the age at marriage. Higher the education of women greater the chances of their being career women. Higher education is more rational. Higher education more selective in the exposure to mass media of communication. Higher education more the accessibility to health services. Higher education more the practice of family planning practices. Higher the education of the parents the higher their aspirations about the education of their children. Higher the education of the couple greater the chances of shifting to nuclear families. Higher the education of the couples the higher their mobility orientation.

3. Give a clear explanation of why we should expect the proposed relationships to exist. For example higher education higher the age at marriage. One could build up the argument like this: For purposes of getting high levels of education, the youngsters spend about 16 years of their life in educational institutions. Let us say they complete their education at the age of 22 years. After completing education they spend 2-3 years on establishing themselves in their careers. During this period continue deferring their marriage. By the time they decide about their marriage they are about 25 years. Compare this age at marriage with the age at marriage of 16 years. Obviously, with this higher age at marriage, there is a reduction in the reproductive period of women. Similarly, we can develop logic in support of other proposed relationships.

4.   Make an inventory of propositions. The proposed relationships under item 2 about could be the examples of propositions.

5.   Arrange these propositions in sequential order. These propositions can be arranged sequentially

TOPIC
16

CRITERIA FOR GOOD MEASUREMENT

The scales developed could often be imperfect and errors are prone to occur in the measurement of attitudinal variables. The use of better instruments will ensure more accuracy in results, which in turn, will enhance the scientific quality of the research. Hence, in some way, we need to assess the "goodness" of the measure developed.

What should be the characteristics of a good measurement? An intuitive answer to this question is that the tool should be an accurate indicator of what we are interested in measuring. In addition, it should be easy and efficient to use. There are three major criteria for evaluating a measurement tool:

- *Validity,*
- *Reliability, and*
- *Sensitivity.*

Validity

Validity is the ability of an instrument (for example measuring an attitude) to measure what it is supposed to measure. That is, when we ask a set of questions (i.e. develop a measuring instrument) with the hope that we are tapping the concept, how can we be reasonably certain that we are indeed measuring the concept we set out to do and not something else? There is no quick answer.

Researchers have attempted to assess validity in different ways, including asking questions such as "Is there consensus among my colleagues that my attitude scale measures what it is supposed to measure?" and "Does my measure correlate with others' measures of the 'same' concept?" and "Does the behavior expected from my measure predict the actual observed behavior?" Researchers expect the answers to provide some evidence of a measure's validity.

What is relevant depends on the nature of the research problem and the researcher's judgment. One way to approach this question is to organize the answer according to measure-relevant types of validity. One widely accepted classification consists of three major types of validity:

(1)   Content validity,

(2)   Criterion-related validity, and

(3)   Construct validity.

(1)   Content Validity

The content validity of a measuring instrument (the composite of measurement scales) is the extent to which it provides adequate coverage of the investigative questions guiding the study. If the instrument contains a representative sample of the universe of the subject matter of interest, then the content validity is good. To evaluate the content validity of an instrument, one must first agree on what dimensions and elements constitute adequate coverage. To put it differently, content validity is a function of how well the dimensions and elements of a concept have been delineated. Look at the concept of *feminism* which implies a person's commitment to a set of beliefs creating full equality between men and women in areas of the arts, intellectual pursuits, family, work, politics, and authority relations. Does this definition provide adequate coverage of the different dimensions of the concept? Then we have the following two questions to measure *feminism*:

1.   Should men and women get equal pay for equal work?

2.   Should men and women share household tasks?

These two questions do not provide coverage to all the dimensions delineated earlier. It definitely falls short of adequate content validity for measuring *feminism.*

A panel of persons to judge how well the instrument meets the standard can attest to the content validity of the instrument. A panel independently assesses the test items for a performance test. It judges each item to be essential, useful but not essential, or not necessary in assessing the performance of relevant behavior.

Face validity is considered as a basic and very minimum index of content validity. Face validity indicates that the items that are intended to measure a concept do on the face of it look like they measure the concept. For example, a few people would accept a measure of college students' math's ability using a question that asked students: 2 + 2 =? This is not a valid measure of college-level math ability on the face of it. Nevertheless, it is a subjective agreement among professionals that a scale logically appears to reflect accurately what it is supposed to measure. When it appears evident to experts that the measure provides adequate coverage of the concept, a measure has face validity.

(2) Criterion-Related Validity

Criterion validity uses some standard or criterion to indicate a construct accurately. The validity of an indicator is verified by comparing it with another measure of the same construct in which research has confidence. There are two subtypes of this kind of validity.

Concurrent validity: To have concurrent validity, an indicator must be associated with a preexisting indicator that is judged to be valid. For example, we create a new test to measure intelligence. For it to be concurrently valid, it should be highly associated with existing IQ tests (assuming the same definition of intelligence is used). It means that most people who score high on the old measure should also score high on the new one, and vice versa. The two measures may not be perfectly associated, but if they measure the same or a similar construct, it is logical for them to yield similar results.

Predictive validity:

Criterion validity whereby an indicator predicts future events that are logically related to a construct is called predictive validity. It cannot be used for all measures. The measure and the action predicted must be distinct from but indicate the same construct. Predictive measurement validity should not be confused with prediction in hypothesis testing, where one variable predicts a different variable in the future.

Look at the scholastic assessment tests being given to candidates seeking admission in different subjects. These are supposed to measure the scholastic aptitude of the candidates – the ability to perform in the institution as well as in the subject. If this test has high predictive validity, then candidates who get a high test score will subsequently do well in their subjects. If students with high scores perform the same as students with an average or low score, then the test has low predictive validity.

(3) Construct Validity

Construct validity is for measures with multiple indicators. It addresses the question: If the measure is valid, do the various indicators operate an inconsistent manner? It requires a definition with clearly specified conceptual boundaries. In order to evaluate construct validity, we consider both theory and the measuring instrument being used. This is assessed through convergent validity and discriminant validity.

Convergent Validity: This kind of validity applies when multiple indicators converge or are associated with one another. Convergent validity means that multiple measures of the same construct hang together or operate in similar ways. For example, we construct "education" by asking people how much education they have completed, looking at their institutional records, and asking people to complete a test of school-level knowledge. If the measures do not converge (i.e. people who claim to have a college degree but have no record of attending college, or those with college degree perform no better than high school dropouts on the test), then our test has weak convergent validity and we should not combine all three indicators into one measure.

Discriminant Validity: Also called divergent validity, discriminant validity is the opposite of convergent validity. It means that the indicators of one construct hang together or converge, but also diverge or are negatively associated with opposing constructs. It says that if two constructs A and B are very different, then measures of A and B should not be associated. For example, we have 10 items that measure political conservatism. People answer all 10 in similar ways. But we have also put 5 questions in the same questionnaire that measure political liberalism. Our measure of conservatism has discriminant validity if the 10 conservatism items hang together and are negatively associated with 5 liberalism ones.

———————

TOPIC
17

WRITING INTRODUCTION IN RESEARCH THESIS/PAPER

What is the function of the Introduction section?

Put simply, the Introduction should answer the question 'Why:' why you choose that topic for research; why it is important; why you adopted a particular method or approach; and so on. You can also think of the Introduction as the section that points out the gap in knowledge that the rest of the paper will fill, or the section in which you define and claim your territory within the broad area of research.

The other job the Introduction should do is to give some background information and set the context. You can do this by describing the research problem you considered or the research question you asked (in the main body of the paper, you will offer the solution to the problem or the answer to the question) and by briefly reviewing any other solutions or approaches that have been tried in the past.

Remember that a thesis or a dissertation usually has a separate chapter titled 'Review of literature,' but a research paper has no such section; instead, the Introduction includes a review in brief.

Now that you have given the background and set the context, the last part of the Introduction should specify the objectives of the experiment or analysis of the study described in the paper. This concluding part of the Introduction should include specific details or the exact question(s) to be answered later in the paper.

The 4-step approach to writing the Introduction section

1. **Provide background information and set the context.**

    This initial part of the Introduction prepares the readers for more detailed and specific information that is given later. The first couple of sentences are typically broad.

Once the first sentence has introduced the broad field, the next sentence can point to the specific area within that broad field.

2.   Introduce the specific topic of your research and explain why it is important.

So now in the following part, you can bring in some statistics to show the importance of the topic or the seriousness of the problem.

Here are some examples:

- A paper on controlling malaria by preventive measures, can mention the number of people affected, the number of person-hours lost, or the cost of treating the disease.

- A paper on developing crops that require little water can mention the frequency of severe droughts or the decrease in crop production because of droughts.

- A paper on more efficient methods of public transport can mention the extent of air pollution due to exhausts from cars and two-wheelers or the shrinking ratio between the number of automobiles and road length.

- Another way to emphasize the importance of the research topic is to highlight the possible benefits from solving the problem or from finding an answer to the question: possible savings, greater production, longer-lasting devices, and so on. This approach emphasizes the positive.

- For example, instead of saying that X dollars are lost because of malaria every year, say that X dollars can be saved annually if malaria is prevented, or X millions of liters of water can be saved by dispensing with irrigation, or X person-hours can be saved in the form of avoided illnesses because of improved air quality or reduced pollution.

3.   Mention past attempts to solve the research problem or to answer the research question.

As mentioned earlier, a formal review of literature is out of place in the Introduction section of a research paper; however, it is appropriate to indicate any earlier relevant research and clarify how your research differs from those attempts. The differences can be simple: you may have repeated the same set of experiments but with a different organism, or elaborated (involving perhaps more sophisticated or advanced analytical instruments) the study with a much larger and diverse sample, or a widely different geographical setting.

4.   Conclude the Introduction by mentioning the specific objectives of your research.

The earlier paragraphs should lead logically to specific objectives of your study. Note that this part of the Introduction gives specific details: for instance, the earlier part of the Introduction may mention the importance of controlling malaria whereas the concluding part will specify what methods of control were used and how they were evaluated. At the same time, avoid too much detail because those belong to the Materials and Methods section of the paper.

A final tip: although the Introduction is the first section of the main text of your paper, you don't have to write that section first. You can write it, or at least revise it after you have written the rest of the paper: this will make the Introduction not only easier to write but also more compelling.

TOPIC
18

TITLE ABSTRACT AND KEYWORDS

- Good research paper titles (typically 10–12 words long) use descriptive terms and phrases that accurately highlight the core content of the paper.

- The abstract should provide a quick and accurate summary of the paper, to help the reader decide whether the rest of the paper is worth reading.

- Keywords ensure that your paper is indexed well by databases and search engines, and thus improve the discoverability of your research. Therefore, keywords should be selected after careful consideration.

More often than not, when researchers set about writing a paper, they spend the most time on the "meat" of the article (the Methods, Results, and Discussion sections). Little thought goes into the title and abstract, while keywords get even lesser attention, often being typed out on-the-spot in a journal's submission system.

Ironically, these three elements—the title, abstract, and keywords—may well hold the key to publication success. A negligent or sloppy attitude towards these three vital elements in the research paper format would be almost equivalent to leaving the accessibility of the research paper up to chance and lucky guessing of target words, indirectly making the effort and time expended on the research and publication process almost null and void.

It could be said that the keywords, title, and abstract operate in a system analogous to a chain reaction. Once the keywords have helped people find the research paper and an effective title has successfully lassoed and drawn in the readers' attention, it is up to the abstract of the research paper to further trigger the readers' interest and maintain their curiosity. This functional advantage alone serves to make an abstract an indispensable component within the research paper format.

However, formulating the abstract of a research paper can be a tedious task, given that abstracts need to be fairly comprehensive, without giving too much away. This is mainly because if readers get all the details of the research paper in the abstract itself, they might be discouraged from reading the entire article.

The title, abstract, and keywords: Why it is important to get them right

The title, abstract, and keywords play a pivotal role in the communication of research. Without them, most papers may never be read or even found by interested readers. Here's why:

- Most electronic search engines, databases, or journal websites will use the words found in your title and abstract, and your list of keywords to decide whether and when to display your paper to interested readers. Thus, these 3 elements enable the dissemination of your research; without them, readers would not be able to find or cite your paper.

- The title and abstract are often the only parts of a paper that are freely available online. Hence, once readers find your paper, they will read through the title and abstract to determine whether or not to purchase a full copy of your paper/continue reading.

- Finally, the abstract is the first section of your paper that journal editors and reviewers read. While busy journal editors may use the abstract to decide whether to send a paper for peer review or reject it outright, reviewers will form their first impression about your paper on reading it.

How to write a good title for a research paper

Journal websites and search engines use the words in research paper titles to categorize and display articles to interested readers, while readers use the title as the first step to determining whether or not to read an article. This is why it is important to know how to write a good title for a research paper. Good research paper titles (typically 10–12 words long) use descriptive terms and phrases that accurately highlight the core content of the paper (e.g., the species studied, the literary work evaluated, or the technology discussed).

How to write a research paper abstract

The abstract should work as a marketing tool. It should help the reader decide "whether there is something in the body of the paper worth reading" by providing a quick and accurate summary of the entire paper, explaining why the research was conducted, what the aims were, how these were met, and what the main findings were.

Types of Abstracts

Generally, between 100 and 300 words in length, abstracts are of different types: descriptive, informative, and structured.

Descriptive abstracts, usually used in the social sciences and humanities, do not give specific information about methods and results.

Informative abstracts are commonly used in the sciences and present information on the background, aim methods, results, and conclusions.

Structured abstracts are essentially informative abstracts divided into a series of headings (e.g., Objective, Method, Results, and Conclusion) and are typically found in medical literature and clinical trial reports.

Write a research paper abstract that is concise and informative. You can follow the same strategy to write a structured abstract; just introduce headings based on the journal/university guidelines.

Here are some steps you can follow to write an effective title:

- Answer the questions: What is my paper about? What techniques/ designs were used? Who/what is studied? What were the results?

- Begin writing the abstract after you have finished writing your paper.

- First, answer the questions "What problem are you trying to solve?" and "What motivated you to do so?" by picking out the major objectives/hypotheses and conclusions from your Introduction and Conclusion sections.

- Next, answer the question "How did you go about achieving your objective?" by selecting key sentences and phrases from your Methods section.

- Now, reveal your findings by listing the major results from your Results section.

- Finally, answer the question "What are the implications of your findings?"

- Arrange the sentences and phrases selected in steps 2, 3, 4, and 5 into a single paragraph in the following sequence: Introduction, Methods, Results, and Conclusions.

Make sure that this paragraph is self-contained and does not include the following:

- Information not present in the paper

- Figures and tables

- Abbreviations

- Literature review or reference citations

- Now, link your sentences.

Ensure that the paragraph is written in the past tense and check that the information flows well, preferably in the following order: purpose, basic study design/techniques used, major findings, conclusions, and implications.

Check that the final abstract

- Contains information that is consistent with that presented in the paper.

- Meets the guidelines of the targeted journal (word limit, type of abstract, etc.)

- Does not contain typographical errors like these that may lead referees and editors to "conclude that the paper is bad and should be rejected."

How to choose appropriate keywords in a research paper

Journals, search engines, and indexing and abstracting services classify papers using keywords. Thus, an accurate list of keywords will ensure correct indexing and help showcase your research to interested groups. This, in turn, will increase the chances of your paper being cited.

Here's how you can go about choosing the right keywords for your paper:

- Read through your paper and list down the terms/phrases that are used repeatedly in the text.
- Ensure that this list includes all your main key terms/phrases and a few additional key phrases.
- Include variants of a term/phrase (e.g., kidney and renal), drug names, procedures, etc.
- Include common abbreviations of terms (e.g., HIV).
- Now, refer to a common vocabulary/term list or indexing standard in your discipline (e.g., GeoRef, ERIC Thesaurus, PsycInfo, ChemWeb, BIOSIS Search Guide, MeSH Thesaurus) and ensure that the terms you have used match those used in these resources.
- Finally, before you submit your article, type your keywords into a search engine and check if the results that show up match the subject of your paper. This will help you determine whether the keywords in your research paper are appropriate for the topic of your article.

Conclusion

While it may be challenging to write effective titles and abstracts and to choose appropriate keywords, there is no denying the fact that it is definitely worth putting in extra time to get these right. After all, these 3 smallest segments of your paper have the potential to significantly impact your chances of getting published, read, and cited.

TOPIC
19

RESEARCH IDEAS AND RESEARCH QUESTIONS

The first and most important step when writing an academic paper is choosing a topic that will advance knowledge and add another building block to the study of science and humanity. As a corollary, it's quite unlikely that a journal editor will accept a paper that does not have a good research question.

A clearly defined research question increases the chances of publication because it gives the researchers greater clarity on developing the study protocol, designing the study, and analyzing the data. A well-defined research question also makes a good initial impression on journal editors/supervisor and peer reviewers. In contrast, a poorly formulated research question can seriously harm your chances of publication, among other adverse effects, because it can easily lead to the perception that the research wasn't well thought out.

Although a single paper can address more than one research question, it is good practice to focus on one primary research question.

So what makes a good research question? While the answer may vary for different types of papers and across disciplines, there are a few overall criteria that you should keep in mind, whether you are writing about Shakespeare, stem cells, or steel processing.

So what?

First and foremost, any research question should pass the "so what?" test: the findings that result from pursuing this question must be important, interesting, and meaningful. Once you have determined the possible outcomes of your research, always ask yourself "So what?"

For example, the research question "Are good

surgeons likely to have long fingers?" is highly unlikely to yield any meaningful knowledge. On the other hand, a targeted question likes.

"Do dexterity tests predict surgical performance among residents?" could help medical training professionals improve training programs in surgical techniques.

NOVELTY IN THE WORK

Lack of originality in findings - in other words, "novelty" - is one of the most common reasons for rejection by journals. Editors of scientific journals stress on novelty and "non-obviousness"; the research question should not already have an obvious or undisputed answer. As some journals reject up to 90% of the papers submitted for publication, it is important to ensure that your paper stands out and provides value in one of the following ways:

- contributes new information that has a real-world application or leads to further lines of research,
- corroborates existing information and extends their generalizability or applicability,
- provides findings that contradict the literature, or
- Critically reviews and analyzes the literature.

Good research questions can arise from critical thinking about current practices and problems, from applying new concepts or methods to old problems, and from ideas that emerge when you teach your subject to others.

Replication is acceptable...sometimes

Not all papers convey absolutely unknown information. For instance, it may be interesting to know whether other researchers' observations can be replicated (especially if the observations were controversial or weak but significant), whether the findings in one population also apply to others, or to clarify known relationships by using new methodologies. A study that validates the findings of other ones while doing away with their limitations can also be very useful.

If your findings are likely to fulfill the above three requirements, you've probably got a worthwhile research question.

FINDING AND FORMULATING GOOD RESEARCH QUESTIONS

Field experience, as well as your own research interests, is obviously important in identifying potential lines of research. However, a thorough review of the existing literature is always critical to make sure your question hasn't become irrelevant. In addition, keep abreast of current developments in the field to avoid doing the very same thing someone else has done (with the enormous amount of scientific output being produced nowadays, this is not an unlikely scenario).

You can also find new research questions from the literature. For instance, the Discussion section of many papers often mentions unresolved questions and additional experiments or studies that can be done. In particular, if the conclusions or generalizability of another study has attracted a lot of controversies, you could attempt to replicate the study in order to validate its results. In sum, a good research question can arise when you identify gaps and weaknesses in the existing literature.

There are a number of other ways of finding a good research question. Attending conferences is one of them. Recent advances in a particular field may be presented at academic conferences or just be known to active researchers in a particular field long before they are published. Thus, participating in such conferences and networking with experts in the field can be a valuable aid in your own research. Invitations for research proposals by funding bodies can also give you specific research ideas that are likely to be approved for funding.

Specific frameworks have been developed to help researchers formulate research questions step by step and factor by factor. Examples of such frameworks are PICOT, PESICO, and FINER. Using these templates can give researchers, especially young researchers, a structured method for brainstorming and finalizing their research questions.

PICOT: Population, Intervention, Control, Outcome, Time Frame

PESICO: Person/problem, Environments, Stakeholders, Intervention, Comparison, Outcomes

FINER: Feasible, Interesting, Novel, Ethical, Relevant

SPICE: Setting, Population, Intervention, Comparison, Evaluation

Conclusion

To conclude, the research question is the most crucial element of any academic paper and the first and most important stage in the publication process. A paper with results that are unoriginal, predictable, or trivial is less likely to be published.

Further, it may be of no use to rewrite or change the presentation of your paper if your study has "used the wrong model or study design, collected data in a manner that would not allow a meaningful examination of the hypothesis, or made too few measurements to permit confident conclusions to be drawn."   Spending time to develop a well-formulated research question will help you avoid these problems.

Key facts

- Research ideas can come from a variety of sources, including informal observations, practical problems, and previous research.

- Research questions expressed in terms of variables and relationships between variables can be suggested by other researchers or generated by asking a series of more general questions of interest.

- It is important to evaluate how interesting a research question is before designing a study and collecting data to answer it. Factors that affect interestingness are the extent to which the answer is in doubt, whether it fills a gap in the research literature, and whether it has important practical implications.

- It is also important to evaluate how feasible a research question will be to answer. Factors that affect feasibility include time, money, technical knowledge and skill, and access to special equipment and research participants.

TOPIC

20

RESEARCH OBJECTIVE(S)

In general, research objectives describe what we expect to achieve by a project. Research objectives are usually expressed in lay terms and are directed to the researcher. Research objectives may be linked with a hypothesis or used as a statement of purpose in a study that does not have a hypothesis. Even if the nature of the research has not been clear to the layperson from the hypotheses, s/he should be able to understand the research from the objectives.

A statement of research objectives can serve to guide the activities of research. Consider the following examples.

Objective: To explore the marginalization of women shown in the text of *A Thousand Splendid Suns.*

Objective: To describe what factors farmers take into account in making such decisions as to whether to adopt a new technology or what crops to grow.

Objective: To develop a budget for reducing pollution by a particular enterprise.

Objective: To describe the habitat of the giant panda in China.

Objective: To explore the narrative structure of *The Kite Runner* by Khaled Hosseini.

In the above examples, the intent of the research is largely descriptive.

These observations might prompt researchers to formulate hypotheses that could be tested in another piece of research. So long as the aim of the research is exploratory, i.e. to describe what is, rather than to test an explanation for what is, a research objective will provide an adequate guide to the research.

How to write my research objectives

Objectives must always be set after having formulated

a good research question. After all, they are to explain the way in which such a question is going to be answered. Objectives are usually headed by infinitive verbs such as:

- To identify
- To establish
- To describe
- To determine
- To estimate
- To develop
- To compare
- To analyze
- To collect
- To explore

1.   To compare the text of *Our Lady of Alice Bhatti* with the text of *A Thousand Splendid Suns*.

2   To analyze the speaking skills of BS 8th Class of the University.

3   To identify the factors associated with a high deficiency in the productive skills of the class of BS English.

TOPIC
21

STATEMENT OF THE PROBLEM

- A statement of the problem is used in research work as a claim that outlines the problem addressed by a study.

- A good research problem should address an existing gap in knowledge in the field and lead to further research.

- To write a persuasive problem statement, you need to describe (a) the ideal, (b), the reality, and (c) the consequences.

Research is a systematic investigative process employed to increase or revise current knowledge by discovering new facts. It can be divided into two general categories:

(1) Basic research, which is inquiry aimed at increasing scientific knowledge, and

(2) Applied research, which is an effort aimed at using basic research for solving problems or developing new processes, products, or techniques.

The first and most important step in any research is to identify and delineate the research problem: that is, what the researcher wants to solve and what questions he/she wishes to answer. A research problem may be defined as an area of concern, a gap in the existing knowledge, or a deviation in the norm or standard that points to the need for further understanding and investigation. Although many problems turn out to have several solutions (the means to close the gap or correct the deviation), difficulties arise where such means are either not obvious or are not immediately available. This then necessitates some research to reach a viable solution.

A statement of the problem is used in research work as a claim that outlines the problem addressed by a study. The statement of the problem briefly addresses the question: What is the problem that the research will address?

What are the goals of a statement of the problem?

1. The ultimate goal of a statement of the problem is to transform a generalized problem (something that bothers you; a perceived lack) into a targeted, well-defined problem; one that can be resolved through focused research and careful decision-making.

2. Writing a statement of the problem should help you clearly identify the purpose of the research project you will propose. Often, the statement of the problem will also serve as the basis for the introductory section of your final proposal, directing your reader's attention quickly to the issues that your proposed project will address and providing the reader with a concise statement of the proposed project itself.

3. A statement of the problem need not be long and elaborate: one page is more than enough for a good statement of the problem.

What are the key characteristics of a statement of the problem?

- A good research problem should have the following characteristics:
- It should address a gap in knowledge.
- It should be significant enough to contribute to the existing body of research
- It should lead to further research
- The problem should render itself to investigation through the collection of data
- It should be of interest to the researcher and suit his/her skills, time, and resources
- The approach towards solving the problem should be ethical

What is the format for writing a statement of the problem?

A persuasive statement of the problem is usually written in three parts:

- **Part A (The ideal):** Describes the desired goal or ideal situation; explains how things should be.

- **Part B (The reality):** Describes a condition that prevents the goal, state, or value in Part A from being achieved or realized at this time; explains how the current situation falls short of the goal or ideal.
- **Part C (The consequences):** Identifies the way you propose to improve the current situation and move it closer to the goal or ideal.

Here is an example:

Example 1

Part A: According to the XY university mission statement, the university seeks to provide students with a safe, healthy learning environment. Dormitories are one important aspect of that learning environment since 55% of XY students live in campus dorms and most of these students spend a significant amount of time working in their dorm rooms. However,

Part B: Students living in dorms A B C, and D currently do not have air conditioning units, and during the hot seasons, it is common for room temperatures to exceed 80 degrees F. Many students report that they are unable to do homework in their dorm rooms. Others report having problems sleeping because of the humidity and temperature. The rooms are not only unhealthy, but they inhibit student productivity and academic achievement.

Part C: In response to this problem, our study proposes to investigate several options for making the dorms more hospitable. We plan to carry out an all-inclusive participatory investigation into options for purchasing air conditioners (university-funded; student-subsidized) and different types of air conditioning systems. We will also consider less expensive ways to mitigate some or all of the problems noted above (such as creating climate-controlled dorm lounges and equipping them with better study areas and computing space).

- **Step 1 (Statement 1):** Describe a goal or desired state of a given situation, phenomenon, etc. This will build the ideal situation (what should be, what is expected or desired)
- **Step 2 (Statement 2):** Describe a condition that prevents the goal, state, or value discussed in Step 1

from being achieved or realized at the present time. This will build the reality or the situation as it is and establishes a gap between what ought to be and what is.

- **Step 3:** Connect steps 1 and 2 using a connecting term such as "but," "however," "unfortunately," or "in spite of."

- **Step 4 (Statement 3):** Using specific details show how the situation in step 2 contains a little promise of improvement unless something is done. Then emphasize the benefits of research by projecting the consequences of possible solutions.

- Here are some examples of how you can write a statement of the problem using the steps mentioned above:

Example 2

Step 1 (Statement 1)

The government of Pakistan has a goal to industrialize the nation by the year 2030 (quote). In this regard, it has encouraged growth-oriented micro and small enterprises that should graduate into medium and large enterprises capable of contributing to the industrialization goal. There are several sessional papers (quote/cite) that contain specific measures to encourage and support small enterprises

Step 2 and 3 (Statement 2)

Despite the said government efforts, there is the slow growth of micro into small enterprises and even slower growth of small into medium scale enterprises (quote, show statistics). The government has officially acknowledged that there exists a "missing middle" in Pakistan meaning that there is a gap between small and large enterprises in the country

Step 4 (Statement 3)

Should the "missing middle" gap persist, the industrialization goal may be difficult to achieve. A need, therefore, arises to investigate why there is a persistent "missing middle" despite government efforts.

Example 3

Statement 1

In order to accomplish their missions, public universities need motivated workforces.

Statement 2

There are, however, frequent and severe disciplinary actions, absenteeism, as well as various forms of unrest in public universities that affect the accomplishment of the set missions. Our preliminary investigation reveals that both non-management and management staff are under-motivated.

Statement 3

Without effective motivational packages and procedures, the said vices are likely to continue and retard the achievement of the universities' missions.

Thus, there is a need to examine the public universities' motivation systems and procedures, which is the aim of the proposed research.

Another approach

Another way to write a statement of the problem is to use a template. Here is a simple template which might be useful for researchers:

There is a problem in _____(e.g. organization or situation where problem is occurring). Despite _____(efforts to prevent or deter), _____(something undesirable or unexpected) is occurring (provide evidence). This problem has negatively affected_____(victims of the problem) because_____. A possible cause of this problem is _____. Perhaps a study which investigates_____ by a _____ (paradigm/method) could help resolve the situation.

TOPIC
22

RESEARCH GAP

The first step of conducting a study is identifying a previously unexplored area of research. Choosing an untapped area in your research field will improve your chances of getting published.

But the big question is: how to decide which research problem should you study? Some researchers have clear ideas about the research problem they want to pursue. However, researchers, particularly those who are at an early stage of their career, find themselves in a fix when they have to zero down on a research topic that is original and innovative. The best way to do this is to identify a gap in existing research in the field, i.e., finding a research gap!

What is a research gap?

Let us begin with understanding what a research gap means. When you read papers or books on topics of your interest, you may realize there are some areas that have significant scope for more research but they have not been tapped by other researchers. In other words, no one has picked up or worked on these ideas. A research gap or a literature gap refers to such unexplored or underexplored areas that have scope for further research.

Why is it important to identify a unique research gap?

Assume that you have completed your research work and published the findings only to find out that another researcher has already published something similar. How devastating would that be! Therefore, it is necessary to find out those problems in your research field which have not been addressed before. Not only would you be investing your funds and resources in the right project but it also increases the chances of your research findings getting published.

Challenges you may face while identifying research gaps

Finding gaps and coming up with original and

innovative topics can be tricky for more than one reason. Here's a list of challenges that you might face while identifying research gaps in your chosen area of study:

1. **The effort of dealing with an enormous amount of information:** There could be a lot of unanswered questions in an area of your interest. So you might get overwhelmed with the number of research gaps you stumble upon and feel confused about which one you should focus on.

2. **The difficulty of searching in an organized manner:** Some researchers may find it difficult to organize the information they have gathered. One can easily lose ideas if they are not noted properly.

3. **Hesitation in questioning established norms:** Some researchers are not confident enough to challenge the existing knowledge in their field and may hesitate to question what others have claimed in their work.

How to identify gaps in the literature

You may wonder what would be the best way to come up with some innovative research questions. Though there is no well-defined process to find a gap in existing knowledge, your curiosity, creativity, imagination, and judgment can help you identify it.

Here are 6 tips to identify research gaps

1. Look for inspiration in published literature

Read books and articles on the topics that you like the most. This will not only help you understand the depth of work done by researchers in your field but also provide an opportunity to ask questions that can lead you to a research gap. You can ask yourself questions like:

- What is the significance of this research to my work or the broader field?

- How can this article help me formulate my research questions?

- Does the author's argument require more clarification?

- What issues or questions has the author not addressed?

- Is there a different perspective that I can consider?

- What other factors could have influenced the results?
- Are the methods or procedures used outdated or no longer considered valid in your field? Is there scope for you to test the findings using more a current approach?
- While reading research articles, you can focus on the Introduction section where the authors explain the importance of their research topic and the gaps they have identified and attempted to fill through their research. Also, look at the directions or suggestions for further research that the authors have made as that could be highly inspiring.
- Read meta-analyses and review papers to learn more about the developments and trends in research over the years in the area of your liking. This will help you get acquainted with the problems that have been researched upon in the past as well as trending queries on those topics that you find interesting.

2. Seek help from your research advisor

Discuss the issues and problems in your field with your research advisor to generate ideas for research. Articulating your ideas and knowing what others think and are working on may help you identify your study area or even identify mistakes in your approach. If you think a question would be interesting to work on, you can discuss it with your advisor and get their suggestions.

3. Use digital tools to seek out popular topics or most cited research papers

To familiarize yourself with the trending queries in your field, you can use digital tools as they can save time and help you cast a wider net in your search for a research gap. Websites that identify the most cited papers in a field along with the emerging branches, influential contributors, publications, and countries in that field can be immensely useful to know which topics are considered important. You can also use Google Trends to learn more about the popular questions related to your research area. This will ease your search for an untapped area in your research field.

4. Check the websites of influential journals

The websites of prominent journals often have a

section called 'key concepts' where experts in an area highlight the central ideas in that field. Reading through this section can help you gain a lot of insights and generate new ideas as well. Moreover, you should also look through the reference section of these papers as it can lead you to important resources on the topic.

5.   Make a note of your queries

It is a good practice to note all the questions that cross your mind while reading any published literature. If possible, you should map the question to the resource it is based on. You can use tables, charts, pictures, or tools to maintain a record. This can help you in the long run when you are developing your idea into a research problem or even when writing your manuscript.

6.   Research each question

1.   Once you have a list of questions that could be explored, you must conduct thorough research on them. What does this mean? Read more about each doubt or query that you have. Find out if other researchers have had similar questions and whether they have found answers to them. This will help you avoid duplication of work.

2.   Your research project is something that you will invest a lot of time in, so make sure it is something that arouses your interest and passion. While you finalize an unprecedented research idea, make sure you consider the time frame available to complete the project as well as other important aspects such as the availability of funds, equipment, and infrastructure. An over-ambitious project may be difficult to accomplish due to time and resources restraints, while research that makes an insufficient contribution may fail to get the approval of your funding committee or the journal's editorial board.

3.   Since there is no specific method to pick out exceptional or interesting research problems. Keep reading and asking questions until you find the extraordinary problem you've been looking for.

TOPIC
23

THE RATIONALE, SCOPE, AND BACKGROUND OF THE STUDY

The rationale of your research is the reason for conducting the study. The rationale should answer the need for conducting the said research. It is a very important part of your publication as it justifies the significance and novelty of the study. That is why it is also referred to as the *justification of the study*. Ideally, your research should be structured as observation, rationale, hypothesis, objectives, methods, results and conclusions.

To write your rationale, you should first write a background on what all research has been done on your study topic. Follow this with 'what is missing' or 'what are the open questions of the study'. Identify the gaps in the literature and emphasize why it is important to address those gaps. This will form the rationale of your study. The rationale should be followed by a hypothesis and objectives.

THE SCOPE OF THE STUDY

The scope of a study explains the extent to which the research area will be explored in the work and specifies the parameters within the study will be operating.

Basically, this means that you will have to define what the study is going to cover and what it is focusing on. Similarly, you also have to define what the study is not going to cover. This will come under the limitations. Generally, the scope of a research paper is followed by its limitations.

As a researcher, you have to be careful when you define your scope or area of focus. Remember that if you broaden the scope too much, you might not be able to do justice to the work or it might take a very long time to complete. Consider the feasibility of your work before you write down the scope. Again, if the scope is too narrow, the findings might not be generalizable.

Typically, the information that you need to include in the scope would cover the following:

1.   General-purpose of the study
2.   The population or sample that you are studying
3.   The duration of the study
4.   The topics or theories that you will discuss
5.   The geographical location covered in the study

Background of your study

While the findings of your study form the foreground of your research, it is equally important to establish the background of your study. A well-written background will provide your study with a context and prompt the readers to read the rest of your paper.

However, most authors struggle with writing the background of the study. Another common problem the authors encounter is distinguishing between the background and the literature review, which are critical aspects of any research paper. The two terms are often used interchangeably; however, they have clearly defined roles. So in this article, I will cover the basics of writing the background and explain how it is different from the literature review.

The background of the study

The background of the study establishes the context of the research. This section explains why this particular research topic is important and essential to understanding the main aspects of the study. Usually, the background forms the first section of a research article/thesis and justifies the need for conducting the study and summarizes what the study aims to achieve.

How to structure the background

In this section, the author usually outlines the historical developments in the literature that led to the current topic of research concisely. If the study is interdisciplinary, it should describe how different disciplines are connected and what aspects of each discipline will be studied.

Additionally, authors should briefly highlight the main developments of their research topic and identify the main gaps that need to be addressed. In other words, this section should give an overview of your study. The section should be organized as:

- What is known about the broad topic?
- What are the gaps or missing links that need to be addressed?
- What is the significance of addressing those gaps?
- What are the rationale and hypotheses of your study?

The background section, therefore, should provide general information about the topic of your research and emphasize the main aims of the study. Please ensure that you only discuss the main and relevant aspects of the studies that have led to your aims. Do not elaborate on them as this should be done in the literature review section. The background section should discuss your findings in a chronological manner to accentuate the progress in the field and the missing points that need to be addressed. The background should be written as a summary of your interpretation of previous research and what your study proposes to accomplish.

How to make the background engaging

- As the background includes a lot of information, it can become a long drag, causing the readers to lose interest. To ensure that your background is engaging, you should try to build a story around the central theme of your research.
- Ensure that the story adheres to the core idea and does not digress into a broad literature review. Each idea should lead to the next so that readers are able to grasp the story and themselves identify the gaps that your study is going to address.
- How to avoid common mistakes in writing the background
- While writing an effective background, you ought to steer clear of some mistakes. The most common mistakes in writing the background include the following:
- Don't write a background that is too long or too short. Focus on including all the important details but write concisely.

- Don't be ambiguous. Writing in a way that does not convey the message to the readers defeats the purpose of the background, so express yourself keeping in mind that the reader does not know your research intimately.

- Don't discuss unrelated themes. Try and center your discussion around the pivotal aspects of your research topic i.e. highlight the gaps in the literature, state the novelty of the study, and the need to conduct the study.

- Don't be disorganized. Not discussing the themes in a chronological manner can confuse the reader about the progress in the field, so try and organize your writing carefully.

How is the background different from the literature review?

Many authors find it difficult to discern the difference between the literature review and the study background. The literature review section should follow the background section, as the second section of your manuscript/thesis. This section basically supports the background section by providing evidence for the proposed hypothesis. This section should be more comprehensive and thoroughly describe all the studies that you have mentioned in the background section. It should also elaborate on all studies that form evidence for the present study and discuss the current trends.

To write this section, you will need to do a thorough literature search on different studies that relate to the broad topic of your research. This will introduce the readers to the area of your research. Following this, you should present a more focused survey of the specific studies that are associated with the precise objective of your study. It would be ideal to organize them thematically and discuss them chronologically so that readers are aware of the evolution and progress in the field. In other words, separate themes should be discussed chronologically to highlight how research in those fields has progressed over time. This will highlight what has been done and what are the future directions that need to be worked upon.

An important thing to consider is that the literature

review should be organized to highlight what research has been done and point out what has been missed. There might be other studies that have tried to fill the gaps in the literature and have been unsuccessful or there might be better ways to address the gaps. Covering these points in the literature review gives the readers a perspective on the significance and the novelty of the study. This can be accomplished by comparing and contrasting previous similar studies to abreast the reader with all the knowledge about the field.

Study background	Literature review
Should be the first section of the study	Should be the section that follows the background of the study
Should provide the context of the study	Should provide a comprehensive overview of broad and specific literature in the field
Should provide a historical perspective and highlight the significance of the study	Should critically highlight the progress of research and gaps that need to be addressed
Should not elaborate on background literature and only summarize it	Should provide a detailed review of the existing literature on the topic

For research papers, it is usual for the background and literature review to be combined and presented together without separate headings. For dissertations, the background and literature review may be presented as separate sections. Ultimately, it is best to check your target journal's instructions before writing the background of your study.

TOPIC

24

SIGNIFICANCE OF THE STUDY

In simple terms, the significance of the study is basically the importance of your research. The significance of a study must be stated in the Introduction section of your research paper. While stating the significance, you must highlight how your research will be beneficial to the development of science and society in general. You can first outline the significance in a broader sense by stating how your research will contribute to the broader problem in your field and gradually narrow it down to demonstrate the specific group that will benefit from your research. While writing the significance of your study, you must answer questions like:

1.   Why should your research be published?

2.   How will this study contribute to the development of your field?

The significance of the study could be simply reflected in the following two questions:

1.   Why should my study be published?

2.   What significant scientific contribution is my study making to my field of research?

Importantly, the significance of the study should also be written with a non-expert in mind.

Writing the Significance of the Study

Here are the tips that may be helpful when writing the significance of the study. These tips will tell you the basic components expected to be seen in the significance of the study content.

1.   Refer to the Problem Statement

In writing the significance of the study, always refer to the statement of the problem. This way, you can clearly define the contribution of your study. To simplify, your research should answer this question, "What are the benefits or advantages of the study based on the statement of the problem?"

If you ask the question "How has the new packaging affected the sales of the product?" then the contribution of your research would probably a packaging style or technology that can help the store increase its sales. Your study should demonstrate that the product's packaging really influences the buyer's perception and affects their purchase decision.

2.   Write it from General to Particular

Determine the specific contribution of your thesis study to society as well as to the individual. Write it deductively, starting from general to specific. Start your significance of the study broadly then narrowing it out to a specific group or person. This is done by looking into the general contribution of your study, such as its importance to society as a whole, then move towards its contribution to individuals as yourself as a researcher.

YOU CAN WRITE SIGNIFICANCE FROM THREE DIMENSIONS

1.   academic significance (field/subject/discipline)

2.   social significance (for common public)

3.   personal significance

PLAGIARISM

Writing a research paper poses challenges in gathering literature and providing evidence for making your paper stronger. Drawing upon previously established ideas and values and adding pertinent information in your paper are necessary steps, but these need to be done with caution without falling into the trap of plagiarism.

What is Plagiarism in Research?

Plagiarism is the unethical practice of using words or ideas (either planned or accidental) of another author/researcher or your own previous works without proper acknowledgment. Considered as a serious academic and intellectual offense, plagiarism can result in highly negative consequences such as paper retractions and loss of author credibility and reputation. It is currently a grave problem in academic publishing and a major reason for the retraction of research papers.

It is thus imperative for researchers to increase their understanding of plagiarism. In some cultures, academic traditions and nuances may not insist on authentication by citing the source of words or ideas. However, this form of validation is a prerequisite in the global academic code of conduct. Non-native English speakers face a higher challenge of communicating their technical content in English as well as complying with ethical rules. The digital age affects plagiarism. Researchers have easy access to material and data on the internet which makes it easy to copy and paste information.

Guard yourself against plagiarism, however accidental it may be. Here are some *guidelines to avoid plagiarism.*

1.   Understand the context

Do not copy-paste the text verbatim from the reference paper. Instead, restate the idea in your own words.

Understand the idea(s) of the reference source well in order to paraphrase correctly.

2.   Quote

Use quotes to indicate that the text has been taken from another paper. The quotes should be exactly the way they appear in the paper you take them from.

3.   Identify what does and does not need to be cited

- Any words or ideas that are not your own but taken from another paper need to be cited.

- Cite Your Own Material—If you are using content from your previous paper, you must cite yourself. Using material you have published before without citation is called self-plagiarism.

- The scientific evidence you gathered after performing your tests should not be cited.

- Facts or common knowledge need not be cited. If unsure, include a reference.

4.   Manage your citations

Maintain records of the sources you refer to. Use citation software like EndNote or Reference Manager to manage the citations used for the paper

Use multiple references for the background information/literature survey. For example, rather than referencing a review, the individual papers should be referred to and cited.

5.   Use plagiarism checkers

You can use various plagiarism detection tools such as iThenticate or eTBLAST to see how much of your paper is plagiarized.

HYPOTHESIS

❖ **In the ordinary context:**

Hypothesis means mere assumptions or suppositions which are to be proved or disproved.

❖ **In the research context:**

A hypothesis is a formal question that is intended to resolve

A supposition or proposed explanation made on the basis of limited evidence as a starting point for further investigation

❖ **An educated guess**

❖ **A tentative point of view**

❖ **A proposition not yet tested**

❖ **A preliminary explanation**

❖ **A preliminary Postulate**

❖ "A hypothesis is a conjectural statement of the relation between two or more variables". (Kerlinger, 1956)

❖ "Hypotheses are single tentative guesses, good hunches – assumed for use in devising theory or planning experiments intended to be given a direct experimental test when possible". (Eric Rogers, 1966)

❖ "Hypothesis is a formal statement that presents the expected relationship between an independent and dependent variable."(Creswell, 1994)

"If a prisoner learns a work skill while in jail, then he is less likely to commit a crime when he is released. "

Purpose

❖ Guides/give direction to the study/investigation

❖ Defines Facts that are relevant and not relevant

❖ Suggests which form of research design is likely to be the most appropriate

❖ Provides a framework for organizing the conclusions of the findings

❖ Limits the research to a specific area

❖ Offers explanations for the relationships between those variables that can be empirically tested

To be complete the hypothesis must include three components

VARIABLES

POPULATION

RELATION

"Increased faculty's efficiency will improve students' result"

Types of Hypothesis

1. UNIVERSAL HYPOTHESIS
2. EXISTENTIAL HYPOTHESIS
3. NULL HYPOTHESIS
4. ALTERNATE HYPOTHESIS
5. RESEARCH HYPOTHESIS

Universal hypothesis

❖ It is one, which denotes that, the stated relationship holds for all specified variables for all times at all places.

❖ For example,

▪ *"if brave soldiers are frequently rewarded for their better performance, they will perform better."*

❖ This relationship held true for all time and all places.

Existential Hypothesis

❖ It is one in which the stated relationship is said to exist for at least one particular case.

❖ For example,

There are at least a few corporate workers who are scrounger and may not perform better despite the fact that he is being awarded suitably for better performance.

Null Hypothesis

❖ Null hypothesis always predicts that there is no relationship between the variables being studied.

❖ The researcher wishes to disapprove of this hypothesis.

❖ It is denoted by H_0

❖ For example:

▪ "There is no relationship between smoking and lung cancer."

Alternate Hypothesis

❖ The alternate hypothesis always predicts that there will be a relationship between the variables being studied.

❖ It is denoted by H_a

DIRECTIONAL HYPOTHESIS & NON-DIRECTIONAL HYPOTHESIS

❖ If the hypothesis simply predicts that there will be a difference between the two groups, then it is a *non-directional hypothesis*. It is non-directional because it predicts that there will be a difference but does not specify how the groups will differ.

▪ "smoking leads to lungs cancer"

❖ If, however, the hypothesis uses so-called comparison terms, such as "greater," less," better," or "worse," then it is a *directional hypothesis*. It is directional because it predicts that there will be a difference between the two groups and it specifies how the two groups will differ

▪ "Smoking will increase the chances of lung cancer in a person than a person who does not smoke."

Research Hypothesis

❖ This type of hypothesis is derived from some type of theory or some observation and examination.

❖ In other words, the hypothesis set upon the basis of theory or prior observation or on logical grounds.

TOPIC
27

METHODS OF DATA COLLECTION

TYPES OF DATA

- **PRIMARY DATA**
- Are those which are collected afresh and for the first time and thus happen to be original in character and known as Primary data.
- **SECONDARY DATA**
- Are those which have been collected by someone else and which have already been passed through the statistical process are known as Secondary data.

COLLECTION OF PRIMARY DATA

- There are several methods of collecting primary data, particularly in surveys and descriptive researches.
- In descriptive research, we obtain primary data either through observation or through direct communication with respondents in one form or another or through personal interviews.

  Methods of data Collecting Primary Data

- **OBSERVATION METHOD:**
- The observation method is a method under which data from the field is collected with the help of observation by the observer or by personally going to the field.
- **ADVANTAGES**
- Subjective bias eliminated

  Researcher gets Current information
- Independent to respondent's variable
- **DISADVANTAGES**

  It is an expensive method
- Time-consuming
- Limited information

Unforeseen factors may interfere with the observational task

- Respondents opinion cannot be recorded on a certain subject

TYPES OF OBSERVATION

- **Structured Observation**
- When observation is done by characterizing the style of recording the observed information, standardized conditions of observation, the definition of the units to be observed, selection of pertinent data of observation then it is a structured observation
- **Unstructured Observation**
- When observation is done without any thought before observation then it is an unstructured observation

TYPES OF OBSERVATION

- **Participant & Non-Participant Observation**
- When the Observer is a member of the group which he is observing then it is Participant Observation. In participant observation

The researcher can record the natural behavior of the group, The researcher can verify the truth of statements given by informants in the context of the questionnaire, Difficult to collect information can obtain through this method but this researcher may lose objectivity of research due to emotional feelings. Prob. of control in observation isn't solved.

- Non-Participant Observation: When an observer is observing people without giving any information to them then it is a non-participant observation

TYPES OF OBSERVATION

- Controlled & Uncontrolled Observation
- When the observation takes place in natural condition i.e. uncontrolled observation. It is done to get a spontaneous picture of life and persons
- When observation takes place according to definite prearranged plans, with the experimental procedure then it is controlled observation generally done in the laboratory under controlled condition.

INTERVIEW METHOD

- This method of collecting data involves presentation or oral-verbal stimuli and reply in terms of oral-verbal responses.
- Interview Method this is Oral Verbal communication. Where interviewer asks questions (which are aimed to get the information required for study) to the respondent

• There are different types of interviews

- **PERSONAL INTERVIEWS:** The interviewer asks questions generally in a face to face contact with the other person or persons.

Types of Personal Interview

- **Structured Interview**

A. Predetermined questions

B. Standardized techniques of recorded Interviewer follows a rigid procedure

C. The time required for such an interview is less than nonstructured manner interview

D. Not necessary for skill or specific knowledge

E. Analysis of data becomes easier

- **Unstructured Interview**

A. No Predetermined questions

B. No Standardized techniques

C. The interviewer has the freedom to ask, omit, add any questions

D. Ask questions without the following the sequence

E. Deep knowledge & skill required

F. Analysis of data is a difficult prescribed manner

Merits of Personal Interview

- Information at greater depth
  The flexibility of restructuring the Questionnaire
- Interviewer by his skill can overcome resistance
- Non-Response generally low

Samples can be controlled more effectively

- Personal information can be obtained

- The interviewer can collect supplementary information about the respondent's personal characteristics and environment which has value in interpreting results

De-Merits of Interview

- Expensive method
- The respondent may give bias information
- Some Executive people are not approachable so data collected may be inadequate

  Takes more time when samples are more
- Systematic errors may occur
- Supervisors have to do complex work of selecting, training and supervising the field staff.

TELEPHONIC INTERVIEWS

- Contacting samples on telephone
- The uncommon method may be used in developed regions

TELEPHONIC INTERVIEWS -MERITS

Flexible compare to mailing method

Faster than other methods

Cheaper than personal interview method

Call-backs are simple and economical also High response than mailing method.

When it is not possible to contact the respondent directly, then the interview is conducted through – Telephone

Replies can be recorded without embarrassment to respondents

The interviewer can explain requirements more easily

No field staff is required

Wider distribution of the sample is possible

TELEPHONIC INTERVIEWS -DEMERITS

- Little time is given to respondents
- The survey is restricted to respondents who have telephones
- Not suitable for an intensive survey where comprehensive answers are

Required

- Bias information may be more
- Very difficult to make questionnaire because it should short and to the point

Other Types

- Focused interviews: attention is focused on the given experience of the respondent and its possible effects.
- Clinical interviews: concerned with broad underlying feelings or motivations or with the course of an individual's life experience, rather than with the effects of the specific experience, as in the case of a focused interview.
- Group interviews: a group of 6 to 8 individuals is interviewed.
- Qualitative and quantitative interviews: divided on the basis of subject matter i.e. whether qualitative or quantitative.
- Individual interviews: The interviewer meets a single person and interviews him.
- Selection interviews: done for the selection of people for certain jobs.
- Depth interviews: it deliberately aims to elicit unconscious as well as other types of material relating especially to personality dynamics and motivations.

QUESTIONNAIRE METHOD

- This method of data collection is quite popular, particularly in the case of big inquiries. The questionnaire is mailed to respondents who are expected to read and understand the questions and write down the reply in the space meant for the purpose of the questionnaire itself.

  The respondents have to answer the questions on their own.

- Questionnaire Method Questionnaire is sent to persons with a request to answer the questions and return the questionnaire Questions are printed in a definite order, mailed to samples who are expected to read that questions understand the questions and write the answers in provided space.

Merits of Questionnaire

- Low cost even the geographical area is large to cover
- Answers are in respondents word so free from bias
- Adequate time to think for answers

  Unapproachable respondents may be conveniently contacted
- Large samples can be used so results are more reliable

Demerits of Questionnaire

- Low rate of return of the duly filled questionnaire

  Can be used when the respondent is educated and cooperative
- It is inflexible
- The omission of some questions
- Difficult to know the expected respondent has filled the form or it is filled by someone else
- Slowest method of data collection

Main aspects of a Questionnaire

1.   General Form

- Structured questionnaire – All questions and answers are specified and comments in the respondents' own words are held to the minimum.
- Unstructured questionnaire- The interviewer is provided with general guidance on the type of information to be collected. He can form his own questions.
- Answers are taken down in respondents own words, at the time recorded On tape

Main aspects of a Questionnaire

2.   Question sequence

- Question sequence should be clear and smoothly moving (relation of one question to another should readily apparent
- First, few questions are important for creating interest in respondents

Mind

- A question which gives stress on memory or of a personal character and wealth should be avoided as opening questions
- The easier question should be at the start of the questionnaire
- General to specific questions should be the sequence of questions

Main aspects of a Questionnaire

3.   Question formation and wording

- The question should easily understand Question should be simple and

Concrete

- Closed questions are easy to handle but this is like fixing the answers in people's mouths. So depending upon the problem for which survey is going on both close-ended and open-ended questions may be asked in the Questionnaire.
- Words having ambiguous meaning should be avoided
- Catchwords, words with emotional connotations, danger words should be avoided.

Essentials of Good Questionnaire

- Good Questionnaire Should Short & simple Questions
- Should arrange in logical sequence (From Easy to difficult one)
- Technical terms should be avoided
- Some control questions which indicate the reliability of the respondent (To Know consumption first expenditure and then weight or quantity of that material)
- Questions affecting the sentiments of the respondents should be avoided
- Adequate space for answers should be provided in the questionnaire
- Provision for uncertainty (do not know, No preference)
- Directions regarding the filling of the questionnaire should be given

- Physical Appearance - Quality of paper, color

SCHEDULE METHOD

It is one of the important methods for the study of social problems.

- Schedules Like Questionnaires but it filled by the enumerator.
- Enumerators are specially appointed for filling the questionnaire
- Enumerators explain the aim and objective to the respondent and fill the answers in the provided space.
- In the words of Thomas Carson Macormic, "The schedule is nothing more than a list of questions which it seems necessary to test the hypothesis ."

Questionnaire V/S Schedule

Generally, send through the mail
No further assistance from sender

- It is a cheaper method
- The non-response is high
- It is not always clear who replies
- Very slow process
- No Personal Contact
- Can be used only when the respondent is educated and cooperative
- Wider distribution of the sample
- Success depends on the quality of the questionnaire
- **The schedule is filled by the enumerator**

  More expensive- Hire and train enumerators
- The non-response is high
- Identity of the responder is known
- Information is collected well in time
- Direct personal contact
- Info can be collected form illiterates also
- No wide distribution of the sample
- Success depends on the honesty and competence of the questionnaire

Other Methods of Data Collection

- **Warranty Cards** - Postcard size cards sent to customers and feedback collected through asking questions on that card
- Distributor or Store Audits - Audits are done by distributor or manufacturer's salesperson. Observation or copying information about inventory in retail shops. A useful method for knowing market share, market size, the effect of in-store promotion.
- **Pantry Audits** - From the observation of pantry of the customer to know purchase habit of the people (which product, of what brand, etc.)

  Questions may be asked at the time of the audit
- **Consumer Panels -** When a pantry audit is done on a regular basis, Daily records of consumption of certain customers. Or repeatedly interviewed at the specific periods to know their consumption.

Other Methods of Data Collection

  Transitory consumer panels – for limited time
- Continuing Consumer panel - For an indefinite period
- Use of Mechanical Device - Eye Cameras to record eyes focus on

  Certain sketch

  Psychogalvanometer to measure body excitement to visual stimulus
- Motion Picture camera to record the movement of the body at the time of

  Purchase
- An audiometer is concerned about TV. Useful to know Channel, program

Preference of people
- Depth Interview - To discover the underlying motives or desires of samples. To explore the needs, feelings of respondents. Skill is required, indirect question or projective techniques are used to know the behavior of the respondent.

- Content Analysis - Analysing contents of documentary material like a newspaper, books magazines about certain characteristics to identify and count

Collection of secondary data

- Data that is already available
- Publications of Central, state, local government
- Technical and trade
  Journals
- Books, Magazines, Newspaper
  Reports & publications of industry, bank, stock exchange
- Reports by research scholars, Universities, economist
- Public Records
- Before using Secondary data researcher must check
  Reliability of the data
- Suitability of data
- Adequacy of data

Selection of appropriate method of data collection

  Nature and scope of the inquiry
- Availability of funds
- Time factor
  Precision required

SAMPLE AND SAMPLING TECHNIQUES

Definition

Sampling is defined as the process of selecting certain members or a subset of the population to make statistical inferences from them and to estimate characteristics of the whole population. Sampling is widely used by researchers in research so that they do not need to research the entire population to collect actionable insights. It is also a time-convenient and a cost-effective method and hence forms the basis of any research design.

For example, if a drug manufacturer would like to research the adverse side effects of a drug on the population of the country, it is close to impossible to be able to conduct a research study that involves everyone. In this case, the researcher decides a sample of people from each demographic and then conducts the research on them which gives them indicative feedback on the behavior of the drug on the population.

Types of Sampling /Sampling Methods

Any research study requires two essential types of sampling. They are:

Probability Sampling: Probability sampling s a sampling method that selects random members of a population by setting a few selection criteria. These selection parameters allow every member to have equal opportunities to be a part of various samples.

Non-probability Sampling: Non-probability sampling method is reliant on a researcher's ability to select members at random. This sampling method is not a fixed or pre-defined selection process which makes it difficult for all elements of a population to have equal opportunities to be included in a sample.

Probability Sampling Methods

Probability Sampling is a sampling technique in which a sample from a larger population is chosen using a method based on the theory of probability. This sampling method considers every member of the population and forms samples on the basis of a fixed process. For example, in a population of 1000 members, each of these members will have 1/1000 chances of being selected to be a part of a sample. It gets rid of bias in the population and gives a fair chance to all members to be included in the sample.

There are 4 types of probability sampling technique:

Simple Random Sampling: One of the best probability sampling techniques that helps in saving time and resources, is the Simple Random Sampling method. It is a trustworthy method of obtaining information where every single member of a population is chosen randomly, merely by chance and each individual has the exact same probability of being chosen to be a part of a sample.

For example, in an organization of 500 employees, if the HR team decides on conducting team building activities, it is highly likely that they would prefer picking chits out of a bowl. In this case, each of the 500 employees has an equal opportunity of being selected.

Cluster Sampling: Cluster sampling is a method where the researchers divide the entire population into sections or clusters that represent a population. Clusters are identified and included in a sample on the basis of defining demographic parameters such as age, location, sex, etc. which makes it extremely easy for a survey creator to derive effective inference from the feedback.

For example, if the government of the United States wishes to evaluate the number of immigrants living in the Mainland US, they can divide it into clusters on the basis of states such as California, Texas, Florida, Massachusetts, Colorado, Hawaii, etc. This way of conducting a survey will be more effective as the results will be organized into states and provide insightful immigration data.

Systematic Sampling: Using a systematic sampling method, members of a sample are chosen at regular intervals of a population. It requires the selection of a starting point for the sample and sample size that can be repeated at regular intervals. This type of sampling method has a predefined interval and hence this sampling technique is the least time-consuming.

For example, a researcher intends to collect a systematic sample of 500 people in a population of 5000. Each element of the population will be numbered from 1-5000 and every 10th individual will be chosen to be a part of the sample (Total population/ Sample Size = 5000/500 = 10).

Stratified Random Sampling: Stratified Random sampling is a method where the population can be divided into smaller groups, that don't overlap but represent the entire population together. While sampling, these groups can be organized and then draw a sample from each group separately.

For example, a researcher looking to analyze the characteristics of people belonging to different annual income divisions will create strata (groups) according to annual family income such as – Less than $20,000, $21,000 – $30,000, $31,000 to $40,000, $41,000 to $50,000, etc. and people belonging to different income groups can be observed to draw conclusions of which income strata have which characteristics. The researchers can analyze which income groups to target and which ones to eliminate in order to create a roadmap that would definitely bear fruitful results.

Use of the Probability Sampling Method

There are multiple uses of the probability sampling method. They are:

Reduce Sample Bias: Using the probability sampling method, the bias in the sample derived from a population is negligible to non-existent. The selection of the sample largely depicts the understanding and the inference of the researcher. Probability sampling leads to higher quality data collection as the population is appropriately represented by the sample.

Diverse Population: When the population is large and diverse, it is important to have adequate representation so that the data is not skewed towards one demographic. For example, if Square would like to understand the people that could their point-of-sale devices, a survey conducted from a sample of people across the US from different industries and socio-economic backgrounds helps.

Create an Accurate Sample: Probability sampling helps the researchers plan and create an accurate sample. This helps to obtain well-defined data.

Types of Sampling: Non-probability Sampling Methods

The non-probability method is a sampling method that involves a collection of feedback on the basis of a researcher or statistician's sample selection capabilities and not on a fixed selection process. In most situations, the output of a survey conducted with a non-probable sample leads to skewed results, which may not totally represent the desired target population. But, there are situations such as the preliminary stages of research or where there are cost constraints for conducting research, where non-probability sampling will be much more effective than the other type.

There are 4 types of non-probability sampling which will explain the purpose of this sampling method in a better manner:

Convenience sampling: This method is dependent on the ease of access to subjects such as surveying customers at a mall or passers-by on a busy street. It is usually termed as convenience sampling, as it's carried out on the basis of how easy is it for a researcher to get in touch with the subjects. Researchers have nearly no authority over selecting elements of the sample and it's purely done on the basis of proximity and not representativeness. This non-probability sampling method is used when there are time and cost limitations in collecting feedback. In situations where there are resource limitations such as the initial stages of research, convenience sampling is used.

For example, startups and NGOs usually conduct convenience sampling at a mall to distribute leaflets of upcoming events or promotion of a cause – they do that by standing at the entrance of the mall and giving out pamphlets randomly.

Judgmental or Purposive Sampling: In judgemental or purposive sampling, the sample is formed by the discretion of the judge purely considering the purpose of study along with the understanding of the target audience. Also known as deliberate sampling, the participants are selected solely on the basis of research requirements and elements who do not suffice the purpose are kept out of the sample. For instance, when researchers want to understand the thought process of people who are interested in studying for their master's degree. The selection criteria will be: "Are you interested in studying for Masters in ...?" and those who respond with a "No" will be excluded from the sample.

Snowball sampling: Snowball sampling is a sampling method that is used in studies that need to be carried out to understand subjects that are difficult to trace. For example, it will be extremely challenging to survey shelterless people or illegal immigrants. In such cases, using the snowball theory, researchers can track a few of that particular category to interview and results will be derived on that basis. This sampling method is implemented in situations where the topic is highly sensitive and not openly discussed such as conducting surveys to gather information about HIV Aids. Not many victims will readily respond to the questions but researchers can contact people they might know or volunteers associated with the cause to get in touch with the victims and collect information.

Quota sampling: In Quota sampling, the selection of members in this sampling technique happens on the basis of a pre-set standard. In this case, as a sample is formed on the basis of specific attributes, the created sample will have the same attributes that are found in the total population. It is an extremely quick method of collecting samples.

Use of the Non-Probability Sampling Method

There are multiple uses of the non-probability sampling method. They are:

Create a hypothesis: The non-probability sampling method is used to create a hypothesis when limited to no prior information is available. This method helps with the immediate return of data and helps to build a base for any further research.

Exploratory research: This sampling technique is widely used when researchers aim at conducting qualitative research, pilot studies or exploratory research.

Budget and time constraints: The non-probability method when there are budget and time constraints and some preliminary data has to be collected. Since the survey design is not rigid, it is easier to pick respondents at random and have them take the survey or questionnaire.

Difference between Probability Sampling and Non-Probability Sampling Methods

We have looked at the different types of sampling methods above and their subtypes. To encapsulate the whole discussion though, the major differences between probability sampling methods and non-probability sampling methods are as below:

	Probability Sampling Methods	Non-Probability Sampling Methods
Definition	Probability Sampling is a sampling technique in which a sample from a larger population is chosen using a method based on the theory of probability.	Non-probability sampling is a sampling technique in which the researcher selects samples based on the subjective judgment of the researcher rather than random selection.
Alternatively Known as	Random sampling method.	Non-random sampling method
Population selection	The population is selected randomly.	The population is selected arbitrarily.
Market Research	The research is conclusive in nature.	The research is exploratory in nature.
Sample	Since there is a method for deciding the	Since the sampling method is arbitrary, the

	sample, the population demographics are conclusively represented.	population demographics representation is almost always skewed.
Time Taken	Take a longer time to conduct since the research design defines the selection parameters before the research study begins.	This type of sampling method is quick since neither the sample or selection criteria of the sample are undefined.
Results	This type of sampling is entirely unbiased and hence the results are unbiased too and conclusive.	This type of sampling is entirely biased and hence the results are biased too rendering the research speculative.
Hypothesis	In probability sampling, there is an underlying hypothesis before the study begins and the objective of this method is to prove the hypothesis.	In non-probability sampling, the hypothesis is derived after conducting the research study.

TOPIC
29

QUALITATIVE AND QUANTITATIVE DATA ANALYSIS METHODS

What is the first thing that comes to mind when we see data? The first instinct is to find patterns, connections, and relationships. We look at the data to find meaning in it.

Similarly, in research, once data is collected, the next step is to get insights from it. For example, if a clothing brand is trying to identify the latest trends among young women, the brand will first reach out to young women and ask them questions relevant to the research objective. After collecting this information, the brand will analyze that data to identify patterns — for example, it may discover that most young women would like to see more variety of jeans.

Data analysis is how researchers go from a mass of data to meaningful insights. There are many different data analysis methods, depending on the type of research. Here are a few methods you can use to analyze quantitative and qualitative data.

It's difficult to analyze bad data. Make sure you're collecting high-quality data

Analyzing Quantitative Data

Data Preparation

The first stage of analyzing data is data preparation, where the aim is to convert raw data into something meaningful and readable. It includes four steps:

Step 1: Data Validation

The purpose of data validation is to find out, as far as possible, whether the data collection was done as per the pre-set standards and without any bias. It is a four-step process, which includes...

Fraud: to infer whether each respondent was actually interviewed or not.

Screening: to make sure that, respondents were chosen as per the research criteria.

Procedure: to check whether the data collection procedure was duly followed.

Completeness: to ensure that the interviewer asked the respondent all the questions, rather than just a few required ones.

To do this, researchers would need to pick a random sample of completed surveys and validate the collected data. (Note that this can be time-consuming for surveys with lots of responses.) For example, imagine a survey with 200 respondents split into 2 cities. The researcher can pick a sample of 20 random respondents from each city. After this, the researcher can reach out to them through email or phone and check their responses to a certain set of questions.

Step 2: Data Editing

Typically, large data sets include errors. For example, respondents may fill fields incorrectly or skip them accidentally. To make sure that there are no such errors, the researcher should conduct basic data checks, check for outliers, and edit the raw research data to identify and clear out any data points that may hamper the accuracy of the results.

For example, an error could be fields that were left empty by respondents. While editing the data, it is important to make sure to remove or fill all the empty fields. (Here are 4 methods to deal with missing data.)

Step 3: Data Coding

This is one of the most important steps in data preparation. It refers to grouping and assigning values to responses from the survey.

For example, if a researcher has interviewed 1,000 people and now wants to find the average age of the respondents, the researcher will create age buckets and categorize the age of each of the respondents as per these codes. (For example, respondents between 13-15 years old would have their age coded as 0, 16-18 as 1, 18-20 as 2, etc.)

Then during analysis, the researcher can deal with

simplified age brackets, rather than a massive range of individual ages.

Quantitative Data Analysis Methods

After these steps, the data is ready for analysis. The two most commonly used quantitative data analysis methods are descriptive statistics and inferential statistics.

Descriptive Statistics

Typically descriptive statistics (also known as descriptive analysis) is the first level of analysis. It helps researchers summarize the data and find patterns. A few commonly used descriptive statistics are:

Mean: the numerical average of a set of values.

Median: midpoint of a set of numerical values.

Mode: most common value among a set of values.

Percentage: used to express how value or group of respondents within the data relates to a larger group of respondents.

Frequency: the number of times a value is found.

Range: the highest and lowest value in a set of values.

Descriptive statistics provide absolute numbers. However, they do not explain the rationale or reasoning behind those numbers. Before applying descriptive statistics, it's important to think about which one is best suited for your research question and what you want to show. For example, a percentage is a good way to show the gender distribution of respondents.

Descriptive statistics are most helpful when the research is limited to the sample and does not need to be generalized to a larger population. For example, if you are comparing the percentage of children vaccinated in two different villages, then descriptive statistics is enough.

Since descriptive analysis is mostly used for analyzing a single variable, it is often called univariate analysis.

Analyzing Qualitative Data

Qualitative data analysis works a little differently from quantitative data, primarily because qualitative data is made up of words, observations, images, and even symbols. Deriving absolute meaning from such data is nearly impossible; hence, it is mostly used for exploratory research. While in quantitative research there is a clear distinction between the data preparation and data analysis stage, analysis for qualitative research often begins as soon as the data is available.

Data Preparation and Basic Data Analysis

Analysis and preparation happen in parallel and include the following steps:

Getting familiar with the data: Since most qualitative data is just words, the researcher should start by reading the data several times to get familiar with it and start looking for basic observations or patterns. This also includes transcribing the data.

Revisiting research objectives: Here, the researcher revisits the research objective and identifies the questions that can be answered through the collected data.

Developing a framework: Also known as coding or indexing, here the researcher identifies broad ideas, concepts, behaviors, or phrases and assigns codes to them. For example, coding age, gender, socio-economic status, and even concepts such as the positive or negative response to a question. Coding is helpful in structuring and labeling the data.

Identifying patterns and connections: Once the data is coded, the research can start identifying themes, looking for the most common responses to questions, identifying data or patterns that can answer research questions, and finding areas that can be explored further.

Qualitative Data Analysis Methods

Several methods are available to analyze qualitative data. The most commonly used data analysis methods are:

Content analysis: This is one of the most common methods to analyze qualitative data. It is used to analyze documented information in the form of texts, media, or even physical items. When to use this method depends on the research questions. Content analysis is usually used to analyze responses from interviewees.

Narrative analysis: This method is used to analyze content from various sources, such as interviews of respondents, observations from the field, or surveys. It focuses on using the stories and experiences shared by people to answer the research questions.

Discourse analysis: Like narrative analysis, discourse analysis is used to analyze interactions with people. However, it focuses on analyzing the social context in which the communication between the researcher and the respondent occurred. Discourse analysis also looks at the respondent's day-to-day environment and uses that information during analysis.

Grounded theory: This refers to using qualitative data to explain why a certain phenomenon happened. It does this by studying a variety of similar cases in different settings and using the data to derive causal explanations. Researchers may alter the explanations or create new ones as they study more cases until they arrive at an explanation that fits all cases.

These methods are the ones used most commonly. However, other data analysis methods, such as **conversational analysis**, are also available.

Data analysis is perhaps the most important component of research. The weak analysis produces inaccurate results that not only hamper the authenticity of the research but also make the findings unusable. It's imperative to choose your data analysis methods carefully to ensure that your findings are insightful and actionable.

TOPIC
30

ETHICAL ISSUES IN RESEARCH

Ethics are norms or standards of behavior that guide moral choices about our behavior and our relationships with others. The goal of ethics in research is to ensure that no one is harmed or suffers adverse consequences from research activities. This objective is usually achieved. However, unethical activities are pervasive and include violating nondisclosure agreements, breaking respondent confidentiality, misrepresenting results, deceiving people, invoicing irregularities, avoiding legal liability, and more.

As discussed earlier, ethical questions are philosophical questions. There is no general agreement among philosophers about the answers to such questions. However, the rights and obligations of individuals are generally dictated by the norms of society. Societal norms are codes of behavior adopted by a group; they suggest what a member of a group ought to do under given circumstances.

Nevertheless, with changing situations people continue differing with each other whereby societal norms may undergo changes. Codes and regulations guide researchers and sponsors. Review boards and peer groups help researchers examine their research proposals for ethical dilemmas. Responsible researchers anticipate ethical dilemmas and attempt to adjust the design, procedures, and protocols during the planning process rather than treating them an afterthought. Ethical research requires personal integrity from the researcher, the project manager, and the research sponsor. Codes of ethics applicable at each stage of the research

Goal

To ensure that no one is harmed or suffers adverse consequences from research activities

Unethical activities

- Violating nondisclosure agreements.
- Breaking respondent confidentiality.
- Misrepresenting results.
- Deceiving people.
- Invoicing irregularities.
- Avoiding legal liability.

Ethical Issues

- Remain to be issued.
- Local norms suggest what ought to be done under the given circumstances.
- Codes of ethics developed to guide researchers and sponsors.
- Review Boards and peer groups help to sort out ethical dilemmas.

Anticipate ethical dilemmas

- Adjust the design, procedures, and protocols accordingly.
- Research ethics require the personal integrity of the researcher, the project manager, and the research sponsor.

Parties in Research

- Mostly three parties:
- The researcher
- The sponsoring client (user)
- The respondent (subject)
- Interaction requires ethical questions.
- Each party expects certain rights and feels certain obligations.

General Rights and Obligations of Parties Concerned

In most research situations, three parties are involved: the researcher, the sponsoring client (user), and the respondent (subject). The interaction of each of these parties with one or both of the other two identifies a series of ethical questions. Consciously or consciously, each party expects certain rights and feels certain obligations towards the other parties. Ethical Treatment of Participants When ethics are discussed in research design, we often think first about protecting the rights of the participant, respondent, or subject. Whether data are gathered in an experiment, interview, observation, or survey, the respondent has any rights to be safeguarded. In general, the research must be designed so that a respondent does not suffer physical harm, discomfort, pain, embarrassment, or loss of privacy. To safeguard against these, the researcher should follow three guidelines;

1.   Explain the study benefits.

2.   Explain respondent rights and protections.

3.   Obtain informed consent.

Benefits:

Whenever direct contact is made with a respondent, the researcher should discuss the study's benefits, being careful to neither overstate nor understate the benefits. An interviewer should begin an introduction with his or her name, the name of the research organization, and a brief description of the purpose and benefit of the research. This puts the respondent at ease, lets them know to whom they are speaking, and motivates them to answer questions truthfully. In short, knowing why one is being asked questions improves cooperation through honest disclosure of purpose. Inducements to participate, financial or otherwise, should not be disproportionate to the task or presented in a fashion that results in coercion.

Sometimes the actual purpose and benefits of the study or experiment must be concealed from the respondents to avoid introducing bias. The need for concealing objectives leads directly to the problem of deception.

TOPIC
31

QUALITATIVE DATA ANALYSIS

Qualitative Data: Definition

Qualitative data is defined as the data that approximates and characterizes.

Qualitative data can be observed and recorded. This data type is non-numerical in nature. This type of data is collected through methods of observations, one-to-one interviews, conducting focus groups and similar methods. Qualitative data in statistics is also known as categorical data. Data can be arranged categorically based on the attributes and properties of a thing or a phenomenon.

Qualitative Data Examples

If the researcher selects a novel/text of the play etc. for the study, the selected text is the data

Qualitative data is also called categorical data since this data can be grouped according to categories.

For example, think of a student reading a paragraph from a book during one of the class sessions. A teacher who is listening to the reading gives feedback on how the child read that paragraph. If the teacher gives feedback based on fluency, intonation, throw of words, clarity in pronunciation without giving a grade to the child, this is considered as an example of qualitative data.

It's pretty easy to understand the difference between qualitative and quantitative data, qualitative data does not include numbers in its definition of traits whereas quantitative data is all about numbers.

- The cake is orange, blue and black in color (qualitative).
- Females have brown, black, blonde, and red hair (qualitative).

Quantitative data is any quantifiable information that can be used for mathematical calculation or statistical analysis. This form of data helps in making real-life decisions based on mathematical derivations. Quantitative data is used to answer questions like how many? how often? how much? This data can be validated and verified.

In order to better understand the concept of qualitative data and quantitative data, it's best to observe examples of particular datasets and how they can be defined.

Following are examples of quantitative data:

- There are 4 cakes and three muffins kept in the basket (quantitative).
- 1 glass of fizzy drink has 97.5 calories (quantitative).

Importance of Qualitative Data

- Qualitative data is important in determining the particular frequency of traits or characteristics. It allows the statistician or the researchers to form parameters through which larger data sets can be observed. Qualitative data provides the means by which observers can quantify the world around them.

- For a researcher, collecting qualitative data helps in answering questions like, who their customers are, what issues or problems they are facing and where do they need to focus their attention so problems or issues are resolved.

- Qualitative data is about the emotions or perceptions of people, what they feel. In quantitative data, these perceptions and emotions are documented. It helps the researcher understand the language their consumers speak. This, in turn, helps the researchers identify and deal with the problem effectively and efficiently.

Qualitative Data Collection Methods- Types of Qualitative Data

Qualitative data collection is exploratory in nature, it involves in-depth analysis and research. Qualitative data collection methods are mainly focused on gaining insights, reasoning, and motivations hence they go deeper in terms of research. Since the qualitative data cannot be measured, this leads to the preference for methods or data collection tools that are structured to a limited extent.

Here are the qualitative data collection methods:

1.   One-to-One Interviews: One of the most commonly used data collection instruments for qualitative research, mainly because of its personal approach. The interviewer or the researcher collects data directly from the interviewee on a one-to-one basis. The interview may be informal and unstructured – conversational. The questions asked are mostly open-ended questions, spontaneous, with the interviewer letting the flow of the interview dictate the next questions to be asked.

2.   Focus groups: This is done in a group discussion setting. The group is limited to 6-10 people and a moderator is assigned to moderate the ongoing discussion.

Depending on the data which is sorted, the members of a group may have something in common. For example, a researcher conducting a study on track runners will choose athletes who are track runners or were track runners and have sufficient knowledge of the subject matter.

3.   Record keeping: This method makes use of the already existing reliable documents and similar sources of information as the data source. This data can be used in the new research. This is similar to going to a library. There one can go over books and other reference material to collect relevant data that can likely be used in the research.

4.   Process of observation: In this qualitative data collection method, the researcher immerses himself/ herself in the setting where his respondents are, and keeps a keen eye on the participants and takes down notes. This is known as the process of observation.

Besides taking notes, other documentation methods, such as video and audio recording, photography and similar methods can be used.

5.   Longitudinal studies: This data collection method is performed on the same data source repeatedly over an extended period of time. It is an observational research method that goes on for a few years and in some cases can go on for even decades. The goal of this data collection method is to find correlations through an empirical study of subjects with common traits.

6.   Case studies: In this method, data is gathered by an in-depth analysis of case studies. The versatility of this method is demonstrated in how this method can be used to analyze both simple and complex subjects. The strength of this method is how judiciously it uses a combination of one or more qualitative data collection methods to draw inferences.

Qualitative Data Analysis

Analyzing your data is vital, as you have spent time and money collecting it in the first place. This is an essential process because you don't want to find yourself in the dark even after putting in so many efforts. However, there are no set ground rules for analyzing qualitative data, it all begins with understanding the two main approaches to qualitative data.

Two Main Approaches to Qualitative Data Analysis

Deductive Approach

The deductive approach involves analyzing qualitative data based on a structure that is predetermined by the researcher. In this case, a researcher can use the questions as a guide for analyzing the data. This approach is quick and easy and can be used when a researcher has a fair idea about the likely responses that he/she is going to receive from the sample population.

Inductive Approach

The inductive approach, on the contrary, is not based on a predetermined structure or set ground rules/framework. This is more time consuming and a thorough approach to qualitative data analysis. The inductive approach is often used when a researcher has very little or no idea of the research phenomenon.

5 Steps to Qualitative Data Analysis

Whether you are looking to analyze qualitative data collected through a one-to-one interview or qualitative data from a survey, these simple steps will ensure a robust data analysis.

Step 1: Arrange your Data

Once you have collected all the data, it is largely unstructured and sometimes makes no sense when looked at a glance. It is, therefore, essential that as a researcher you need to first transcribe the data collected. The first step in analyzing your data is arranging your data systematically.

Arranging data simply means converting all the data into a text format. You can either export the data into a spreadsheet or manually type in the data or choose from any of the computers assisted qualitative data analysis tools.

Step 2: Organize all your Data

After transforming and arranging your data, the immediate next step is to organize your data. There are chances you most likely have a large amount of information that still needs to be arranged in an orderly manner. One great way to organize the data is by going back to your research objectives and then organizing the data based on the questions asked. Arrange your research objective in a table so it appears visually clear. At all costs, avoid temptations of working with unorganized data. You will end up wasting time and there will be no conclusive results obtained.

Step 3: Set a Code to the Data Collected

Setting up proper codes for the collected data takes you a step ahead. Coding is one of the best ways to compress a huge amount of information collected. Coding of qualitative data simply means categorizing and assigning properties and patterns to the collected data. Coding is an important step in qualitative data analysis as you can derive theories from relevant research findings. After assigning codes to your data, you can then begin to build on the patterns to gain in-depth insight into the data that will help make informed decisions.

Step 4: Validate your Data

Validating data is one of the important steps of qualitative data analysis for successful research. Since data is quintessential for research, it is extremely important to ensure that the data is not flawed. Please note that data validation is not just one step in qualitative data analysis, this is a recurring step, that needs to be followed throughout the research process. There are two sides to validating data:

Accuracy of your research design or methods.

Reliability, which is the extent to which the methods produce accurate data consistently.

Step 5: Concluding the Analysis Process

It is important to finally conclude your data, which means, presenting your data in a systematic manner, a report that can be readily used. The report should state the method that you as a researcher used to conduct the research studies, the positives, and negatives and study limitations. In the report, you should also state the suggestions/inferences of your findings and any related area for future research.

Advantages of Qualitative Data

1.   It helps in-depth analysis: Qualitative data collected provide the researchers with an in-depth analysis of subject matters. While collecting qualitative data, the researchers tend to probe the participants and can gather an ample amount of information by asking the right kind of questions. From a series of questions and answers, the data that is collected is used to draw conclusions.

2.   Understand what customers think: Qualitative data helps the researchers to understand the mindset of their customers. The use of qualitative data gives businesses an insight into why a customer purchased a product. Understanding customer language helps research infer the data collected in a more systematic manner.

3.   Rich data: Collected data can be used to conduct research in the future as well. Since the questions asked to collect qualitative data are open-ended questions, respondents are free to express their opinions which leads to collecting more information.

Disadvantages of Qualitative Data

1.   Time-consuming: As collecting qualitative data is more time consuming, fewer people are studies in comparison to collecting quantitative data and unless time and budget allow, the smaller sample size is included.

2.   Not easy to generalize: Since fewer people are studied, it is difficult to generalize the results of that population.

3.   Is dependent on the researcher's skills: This type of data is collected through one-to-one interviews, observations, focus groups, etc. it relies on the researcher's skills and experience to collect information from the sample

TOPIC
32

SURVEY RESEARCH

Survey: Definition

A Survey is defined as a research method used for collecting data from a pre-defined group of respondents to gain information and insights on various topics of interest. Surveys have a variety of purposes and can be carried out in many ways depending on the methodology chosen and the objectives to be achieved.

The data is usually obtained through the use of standardized procedures whose purpose is to ensure that each respondent is able to answer the questions at a level playing field to avoid biased opinions that could influence the outcome of the research or study. A survey involves asking people for information through a questionnaire, which can be distributed on paper, although with the arrival of new technologies it is more common to distribute them using digital media such as social networks, email, QR codes or URLs.

Characteristics of a Survey

The need to observe or research facts about a situation leads us to conduct a survey. As we mentioned at the beginning, a survey is a method of gathering information.

So, what do you need to conduct a survey?

First, a sample, also referred to as the audience, is needed which should consist of a series of survey respondents data with required demographic characteristics, who can relevantly answer your survey questions and provide the best insights. Better the quality of your survey sample, better will be your response quality and better your insights.

Surveys come in many different forms and have a variety of purposes, but they have common underlying characteristics. The basic characteristics of a survey are:

Sample and Sample Determination

A sample is a selection of respondents from a population in such a manner that the sample represents the total population as closely as possible.

The characteristics of a survey sample are:

Determining sample size: Once you have determined your sample, the total number of individuals in that particular sample is the sample size. Selecting a sample size depends on the end objective of your research study. It should consist of a series of survey respondents' data with required demographic characteristics, which can relevantly answer your survey questions and provide the best insights.

Types of sampling: There are two essential types of sampling methods, they are Probability sampling and Non-probability sampling. Although sampling is conducted at the discretion of the researcher, the two methods used in detail, are:

Probability sampling: Probability sampling is a sampling method where the respondent is selected based on the theory of probability. The major characteristic of this method is that each individual in a population has an equal chance of being selected.

Non-probability sampling: Non-probability sampling is a sampling method where the researcher selects a sample of respondents purely on the basis of their own discretion or gut. There is no predefined selection method.

Survey Questions: Questionnaire for your survey

Effective survey questions are the cornerstone for the success of any survey and subsequently, any research study.

The characteristics of the survey questions are as follows:

Data collection: Whether it an email survey, SMS survey, web intercept survey or a mobile app survey, the single common denominator that determines how effectively you are able to collect accurate and complete survey responses is your survey questions and their types.

Fundamental levels of measurement scales: There are

four measurement scales that are fundamental to creating a multiple-choice question in a survey. They are, nominal, ordinal, interval and ratio measurement scales without the fundamentals of which, no multiple-choice questions can be created. Hence, it is important to understand these levels of measurement to be able to create a robust survey.

Use of different question types: Multiple choice questions are the most common type of survey questions, in which, some of the popular question types are: dichotomous question, semantic differential scale question, rank order questions, and rating scale questions. Open-ended questions are used to collect in-depth qualitative data.

Administering the survey

To conduct a survey, it is important to plan the type of survey to ensure you get the optimum number of responses required for your survey. It could be a mix of interviews and survey questions or a questionnaire. Interviews could be telephone interviews, face-to-face interviews, online interviews, and questionnaires can be mall surveys or web surveys. The underlying difference between a survey and a questionnaire is that a questionnaire may or may not be delivered in the form of a survey, but a survey always consists of a questionnaire.

Survey Methods

Survey methodology studies the in-depth sampling of individual units from a population and administering data collection techniques on that sample. It includes instruments or processes that ask different question types to a predefined sample, to conduct data-collection and increase the survey response rate.

The two distinctive member types are in a survey methodology are professionals in the field that focus on empirical survey errors and others that work to design surveys and reduce them. it is therefore both a scientific field and a profession. The primary tasks of a survey methodologist while administering a survey is to identify and create samples, validate test questions, select the mode to administer questions and validate methods for data collection, statistical analysis, and data reporting.

Survey Methods based on Design

Surveys can be administered by the time they take to complete, the two types are:

Cross-sectional studies: Cross-sectional study is defined as an observational research type that analyzes data of variables collected at one given point of time across a sample population. population or a pre-defined subset. This study type is also known as cross-sectional analysis, transverse study or prevalence study. The data gathered in a cross-sectional study is from people who are similar in all variables except the one variable which is under study. This variable remains constant throughout the cross-sectional study. This is unlike a longitudinal study, where variables in the study can change over the course of research.

Longitudinal studies: Longitudinal study is an observational study that employs continuous or repeated measures to follow particular individuals over a prolonged period of time often years or decades. The longitudinal study collects data that is either qualitative or quantitative in nature. In the longitudinal study, a survey creator is not interfering with survey respondents. Survey respondents are observed over a period of time ranging from months to even decades to observe any changes in them or their attitude. For example, a researcher wants to find out which disease affects young boys (in the age group of 10-15) then the researcher will observe the individuals over that period to collect meaningful data.

Correlational studies: Correlational study is a non-experimental type of research design where two distinct variables are studied and statistical analysis is run to study the relationship between them without the interference of external "variables". This study aims to understand the change and level of change in one of the two variables in the study if the other variable changes. It is close to impossible to understand in this research method though, that, the cause of change in either variable. For example, if an ice-cream truck has a jingle that can be loudly heard, people start understanding which ice-cream truck is in the neighborhood and how far it is from the location of the person in question.

Survey Methods based on Distribution

There are different ways of survey distribution Some of the most commonly used methods are:

Email: Sending out an email is the easiest way of conducting a survey. The respondents are targeted and there is a higher chance of response due to the respondents already knowing about your brand.

Buy respondents: Buying a sample helps achieve a lot of the response criteria because the people who are being asked to respond have signed up to do so and the qualifying criteria for the research study are met.

Embed survey on the website: Embedding a survey on a website ensures that the number of responses is very high. This can be done while the person enters the website or is exiting it. A non-intrusive method of collecting feedback is important to achieve a higher number of responses. The responses received are also honest due to the high brand recall value and the responses are quick to collect and analyze due to them being in a digital format.

Post to the social network: Posting on social networks is another effective way of collecting responses. The survey can be posted as a link and people that follow the brand can take a survey. This method is used when there is no upper cap on the number of survey responses required and is the easiest and fastest way of eliciting responses.

QR code: QR codes store the URL for the survey. You can print/publish this code in magazines, on signs, business cards, or on just about any object/medium. Users with a camera phone equipped with the correct reader application can scan the image of the QR Code to open the survey in the phone's browser.

SMS: Using SMS surveys are another quick way to collect feedback. This method can be used in the case of quick responses and when the survey is simple, straightforward and not too long. This method is used to increase the open and response rate of collecting feedback.

Surveys can be distributed using one, some or a mix of the above methods depending on the basis of the research objective and the resources being used for any particular survey. Many factors play a part in the mode of distribution of surveys like cost, research study type, the flexibility of questions, time to collect responses, statistical analysis to be run on data and willingness of the respondent to take part in the survey.

You can conduct a telephone or email survey and then make a selection of respondents for a face-to-face interview. Survey data are sometimes also obtained through questionnaires filled out by respondents in groups, for example, a school class or a group of shoppers in a shopping center.

Survey Data Collection

The methods used to collect survey data have evolved with time. Researchers have increasingly moved away from paper surveys to using smart, online surveys. Each survey data collection method has its pros and cons and the researcher has to in most cases, use different methods to collect the requisite data from a sample.

The survey response rates of each of these methods vary as multiple factors like time, interest, incentive, etc. play a role in the data collection process.

In the section above, we have looked at survey data collection methods on the basis of design, cross-sectional surveys, and longitudinal surveys. In this method, we will look at the four main survey data collection methods on the basis of their actual implementation. They are:

Online surveys: Online surveys have now become the most widely used survey data collection method. This method is now widely being used because the reach of the surveys has increased to wherever there is internet access, which is everywhere. There is no limit to the types of questions that can be asked in online surveys and the data collection and data analysis are now structured and easy to manage. The survey response rate of online surveys is very high compared to other survey mediums.

Telephone surveys: Telephone surveys are a cheaper method than face-to-face surveys and less-time consuming too. Contacting respondents via the telephonic medium requires less effort and manpower but the survey response rate could be debated as respondents aren't very trusting to give out information on the call. In this survey data collection method, the researcher also has less scope to digress from the survey flow.

Face-to-face surveys: Face-to-face surveys are on the most widely used methods of survey data collection. The survey response rate in this survey data collection method is always higher because the respondent trusts the researcher since it is in-person. The survey design in this research method is planned well in advance but there is so scope to digress to collect in-depth data.

Paper surveys: The least used survey data collection method that is now being used mostly in field research are paper surveys. Since they are logistically tough to manage and tough to analyze, researchers and organizations are moving away from using this method. These surveys can be used where laptops, computers, and tablets cannot go and hence they use the age-old method of data collection; pen and paper.

Survey Data Analysis

When you conduct a survey, you must have access to its analytics. While manual surveys based on pen and paper or excel sheets require additional man-power to be analyzed by experienced data analysts, it becomes much simpler when using an online survey platform.

Statistical analysis can be conducted on this survey data to make sense of all the data that has been collected. There are multiple methods of survey data analysis, mostly for what is quantitative data. Most of the commonly used types are:

Cross-tabulation: Cross-tabulation is one of the simplest statistical analysis tools that use a basic tabulation framework to make sense of data. Raw survey data can be daunting but structuring that data into a table helps draw parallels between different research parameters. It involves data that is mutually exclusive to each other.

Trend analysis: Trend analysis provides the ability to look at survey-data over a long period of time. This method of statistical analysis of survey data helps plot aggregated response data over time which can be used to draw conclusions about the change in respondent perception over time.

MaxDiff analysis: The MaxDiff analysis method is used to understand customer preferences across multiple parameters. For example, a product's pricing, features, marketing, etc. become the basis for maxdiff analysis. In a simplistic form, this method is also called the "best-worst" method. This method is similar to conjoint analysis but is much easier to implement.

Conjoint analysis: Conjoint analysis is an advanced statistical research method that aims to understand the choices a person makes in selecting a product or service. This method offers in-depth insights into what is important to a customer and what parameters sway their purchasing decisions.

TURF analysis: TURF Analysis or Total Unduplicated Reach and Frequency Analysis, is a statistical research methodology that assesses the total market reach of a product or service or a mix of both. This method is widely used by organizations to understand at what frequency is their messaging reaching the audience and if that needs tweaking. TURF Analysis is widely used to formulate and measure the success of go-to-market strategies.

Gap analysis: Gap analysis uses a side-by-side matrix question type that helps measure the difference between expected performance and actual performance. This statistical method for survey data helps understand the things that have to be done to move performance from actual to planned performance.

SWOT analysis: SWOT analysis, another widely used statistical method organizes survey data into data that represents strength, weaknesses, opportunities, and threats of an organization or product or service that provides a holistic picture about competition. This method helps to create effective business strategies.

Text analysis: Text analysis is an advanced statistical method where intelligent tools make sense of and quantify or fashion qualitative and open-ended data into easily understandable data. This method is used when the survey data is unstructured.

What is an Online Survey?

An online survey is a set of structured questions that

the respondent completes over the internet, generally through filling out a form. An online survey is an easier way to reach out to the respondents as it is less time consuming than the traditional way of gathering information through one to one interaction and also less expensive.

Online surveys can differ in length and format used. The data is collected and stored in a database which is later evaluated by an expert in the field.

As an incentive for respondents to fill out online surveys, businesses offer them rewards like gift cards, reward points that they can redeem for goods or services later, free airline miles, discounts at gas stations, etc.

Online surveys with rewards are a win-win situation for both, businesses and respondents. The businesses or organizations get valuable data from a controlled environment, for the research, and for the respondents, it's a humble gesture from businesses to participate in the survey and spends their valuable time.

What are the Advantages of an Online Survey?

Online surveys are one of the less time-consuming methods to reach out to your target audiences, but that's not the only advantage of an online survey, let us understand what are the other advantages of using online survey:

Accuracy: In online surveys, usually the margin of error is reduced, as the respondents register their responses by easy selection buttons. Tradition methods require human interference and according to a study, human interference increases the margin of error by 10%.

Easy and quick to analyze: Since all the responses are registered online, it is extremely easy and quick to analyze the data in real-time. It is also quick to draw inferences and share the result.

Ease of participation: In this new age technology-oriented universe, most people on this planet have access to the internet. Respondents prefer receiving the survey over the email. Ease of participation greatly increases as the respondents can choose a suitable time and place, according to their convenience to register their responses.

Great branding exercise: While designing the survey

online, organizations or businesses have this opportunity to design their survey to align with their brand. Using logos and similar brand language (color and fonts) in the survey, gives an advantage to the businesses as respondents are able to connect better with the brand.

Respondents can be honest and flexible at the same time: According to a study researchers have found increased participation by respondents when deployed with online surveys rather than answering lengthy questions. By designing surveys that ask relevant questions, respondents are honest with their answers and can skip the questions or respondents to a more neutral option in the survey, increasing their flexibility to respond.

Who Conducts the Surveys?

The person who conducts a survey is usually called an interviewer or a pollster, whether they make a phone call, appear at the door of your house or at the mall to do their work. Those who attend a panel, or online panel, can also be called the administrator.

Those who are responsible for performing this task preferably should be open people, patients, who have the ability to approach strangers to engage in a conversation and carry out the survey according to the instructions received.

These people are not those who bear the full responsibility of conducting a survey, there are also those who are dedicated to design it, determine the sample, write the questions, supervise the collection and analysis of the data and write the corresponding reports of the results obtained.

On the other hand, if you are conducting an online survey, all you have to do is create, send and automatically analyze the surveys from respondents. A research analyst is typically the person who creates and sends out these online surveys to be answered by respondents.

How is a Survey Created and Designed?

As explained before, a survey usually has its beginnings when a person, company or organization faces a need for information and there is no existing data that is sufficient. Take into account the following recommendations:

Define objective: The survey would have no meaning if the objective and the end result was not planned before administering the survey. The methodology has to be planned for and broken down into actionable milestones as well as the sample planned for. Appropriate survey distribution methods for these samples also have to be put in place right at the outset.

The number of questions: The number of questions used in a research study is dependent on the end objective of the research. It is important to note, not to ask redundant questions or questions where the answers are already known. The length of the survey has to be dictated only by the core data metrics that have to be collected.

Simple language: One factor that can cause a high survey dropout rate is if the complex language is used in a survey or if the respondent finds the language uncomfortable to understand. Therefore, it is imperative to use easily understandable text in the survey.

Question types: Multiple types of questions can be used in a survey. It is important to use the question types that offer the most value to the research whilst being the easiest to understand and answer to a respondent. Using close-ended questions like the Net Promoter Score (NPS) questions or multiple-choice questions help increase the survey response rate.

Consistent scales: If you use rating scale questions, make sure that the scales are consistent throughout the survey. Using scales from -5 to +5 in one question and -3 to +3 in another question may confuse a respondent.

Survey logic: Survey logic is one of the most important aspects of the survey design. If the logic is flawed, respondents are put off from continuing with the survey. Logic has to be applied and tested to ensure that on selecting an option, only the next logical question shows up.

Apart from the above-mentioned points, it is important to remember that when you ask survey questions based on past events and experience, you will have to rely and trust on the memory of the respondents. This is a single "assumed" variable in any survey that seeks to understand user behavior through past experiences and events.

TOPIC
33

E-MAIL AND INTERNET SURVEYS

E-Mail Surveys

Questionnaires can be distributed via e-mail. E-mail is a relatively new method of communication, and many individuals cannot be reached this way. However, certain projects lend themselves to, such as internal surveys of employees or satisfaction surveys of retail buyers who regularly deal with an organization via e-mail.

The benefits of an e-mail include the speed of distribution, lower distribution, and processing cost, faster turnaround time, more flexibility, and less handling of paper questionnaires. Many respondents may feel that they can be more candid in e-mail than in person or on the telephone, for the same reason they are candid on other self-administered questionnaires. In many organizations, the employees know that their e-mails are not secure, that "eves-dropping" by a supervisor could occur. Further maintaining the respondent's anonymity is difficult, because a reply to an e-mail message typically includes the sender's address. Researchers designing e-mail surveys should assure respondents that their responses will be confidential.

Not all e-mail systems have the same capacity: some handle color and graphics well; others are limited to text. The extensive differences in the capabilities of respondents' computers and email software limit the types of questions and the layout of the questionnaire.

Internet Surveys

An internet survey is a self-administered questionnaire posted on a Web site. Respondents provide answers to questions displayed on the screen by highlighting a phrase, clicking an icon, or keying in an answer. Like any other survey, Internet surveys have both advantages and disadvantages.

Advantages of Internet Surveys

Speed and Cost Effectiveness:

Internet survey allows the researcher to reach a large audience (possible a global one), to personalize the individual messages, and to secure confidential answers quickly and cost-effectively. The computer to computer self-administered questionnaire eliminates the cost of paper, postage, data entry, and other administrative costs. Once an Internet questionnaire has been developed, the incremental cost of reaching additional respondents is marginal. Hence samples can be larger than with interviews or other types of self-administered questionnaires.

Visual Appeal and Interactivity:

Surveys conducted on Internet can be interactive. The researcher can use more sophisticated lines of questioning based on the respondents' prior answers. Many of this interactive survey utilizes color, sound, and animation, which may help to increase the respondents' cooperation and willingness to spend more time answering questions. The Internet is an excellent medium for the presentation of visual materials, such as photographs or drawings of product prototypes, advertisements, and movie trailers

Respondent Participation and Cooperation:

Participation in some Internet surveys occurs because computer users intentionally navigate to a particular Web site where questions are displayed. In some instances individuals expect to encounter a survey at a Web site; in other cases, it is totally unexpected.

Accurate Real-Time Data Capture: The computer to computer nature of Internet surveys means that each respondent's answers are entered directly into the researcher's computer as soon as the questionnaire is submitted. In addition, the questionnaire software may be programmed to reject improper data entry.

Real-time data capture allows for real-time data analysis. A researcher can review up-to-the-minute sample size counts and tabulation data from an Internet survey in real-time.

Callbacks: When the sample for the Internet survey is drawn from a consumer panel, it is easy to recontact those who have not yet completed the questionnaire. Computer software can also identify the passwords of those respondents who completed only a portion of the questionnaire and send those people customized messages.

Personalized and Flexible Questioning: There is no interviewer in Internet surveys but the respondent interacts directly with the software on a Web site. In other words, the computer program asks questions in a sequence determined by a respondent's previous answer. The questions appear on the computer screen, and answers are recorded by simply pressing a key clicking an icon, thus immediately entering the data into the computer's memory. This ability to sequence the question based on previous responses is a major advantage of computer-assisted surveys.

Respondent Anonymity: Respondents are more likely to provide sensitive information when they can remain anonymous. The anonymity of the Internet encourages respondents to provide honest answers to sensitive questions.

Most respondents do not feel threatening to enter information into computing because of the absence of the interviewer. They may be assured that no human will ever see their individual responses.

Response Rate: Response rate can be increased by sending e-mail friendly reminders.

Disadvantages of Internet Surveys

All People cannot participate: Many people in the general public cannot access to the Internet. And, all people with Internet access do not have the same level of technology. Many lack powerful computers or software that is compatible with advanced features programmed into many Internet questionnaires.

Some individuals have minimal computer skills. They may not know how to navigate through and provide answers to an Internet questionnaire.

No Physical Incentive: Unlike mail surveys, Internet surveys do not offer the opportunity to send a physical incentive to the respondent.

SELECTING THE APPROPRIATE SURVEY RESEARCH DESIGN

The choice of communication method is not as complicated as it might appear. By comparing the research objectives with the strengths and weaknesses of each method, the researcher will be able to choose one that is suited to the needs. Nevertheless, there no "best" form of survey. Each has advantages and disadvantages. A researcher who must ask highly confidential questions ay conduct a mail survey, thus trading off the speed of data collection to avoid any possibility of interviewer bias.

To determine the appropriate technique, the researcher must ask questions such as "Is the assistance of an interviewer necessary? Are respondents likely to be interested in the issues being investigated? Will cooperation be easily attained? How quickly the information is needed? Will the study require a ling complex questionnaire? How large is the budget?" The criteria – cost, speed, anonymity, and the like – may be different for each project.

If none of the choices turns out to be a particularly good fit, it is possible to combine the best characteristics of two or more alternatives into a *mixed-mode.* Although this decision will incur the costs of the combined modes, the flexibility of tailoring a method to the unique need of the project is often an acceptable trade-off.

TOPIC
34

FIELD RESEARCH

Field research is defined as a qualitative method of data collection that aims to observe, interact and understand people while they are in a natural environment. For example, nature conservationists observe the behavior of animals in their natural surroundings and the way they react to certain scenarios. In the same way, social scientists conducting field research may conduct interviews or observe people from a distance to understand how they behave in a social environment and how they react to situations around them.

Field research encompasses a diverse range of social research methods including direct observation, limited participation, analysis of documents and other information, informal interviews, surveys, etc. Although field research is generally characterized as qualitative research, it often involves multiple aspects of quantitative research in it.

Field research typically begins in a specific setting although the end objective of the study is to observe and analyze the specific behavior of a subject in that setting. The cause and effect of a certain behavior, though, is tough to analyze due to the presence of multiple variables in a natural environment. Most of the data collection is based not entirely on cause and effect but mostly on correlation. While field research looks for correlation, the small sample size makes it difficult to establish a causal relationship between two or more variables.

Methods of Field Research

Field research is typically conducted in 5 distinctive methods. They are:

Direct Observation

In this method, the data is collected via an observational method or subjects in a natural environment. In this method, the behavior or outcome of the situation is not interfered with in any way by the researcher. The advantage of direct observation is that it offers contextual data on people, situations, interactions, and surroundings. This method of field research is widely used in a public setting or environment but not in a private environment as it raises an ethical dilemma.

Participant Observation

In this method of field research, the researcher is deeply involved in the research process, not just purely as an observer, but also as a participant. This method too is conducted in a natural environment but the only difference is the researcher gets involved in the discussions and can mould the direction of the discussions. In this method, researchers live in a comfortable environment with the participants of the research, to make them comfortable and open up to in-depth discussions.

Ethnography

Ethnography is an expanded observation of social research and social perspective and the cultural values of an entire social setting. In ethnography, entire communities are observed objectively. For example, if a researcher would like to understand how an Amazon tribe lives their life and operates, he/she may choose to observe them or live amongst them and silently observe their day-to-day behavior.

Qualitative Interviews

Qualitative interviews are close-ended questions that are asked directly to the research subjects. The qualitative interviews could be informal and conversational, semi-structured, standardized and open-ended or a mix of all the above three. This provides a wealth of data to the researcher that they can sort through. This also helps collect relational data. This method of field research can use a mix of one-on-one interviews, focus groups, and text analysis.

Case Study

A case study research is an in-depth analysis of a person, situation or event. This method may look difficult to operate; however, it is one of the simplest ways of conducting research as it involves a deep dive and thorough understanding of the data collection methods and inferring the data.

Steps in Conducting Field Research

Due to the nature of field research, the magnitude of timelines and costs involved, field research can be very tough to plan, implement and measure. Some basic steps in the management of field research are:

Build the Right Team: To be able to conduct field research, having the right team is important. The role of the researcher and any ancillary team members is very important and defining the tasks they have to carry out with defined relevant milestones is important. It is important that upper management is vested in the field research for its success.

Recruiting People for the Study: The success of the field research depends on the people that the study is being conducted on. Using sampling methods, it is important to derive the people that will be a part of the study.

Data Collection Methodology: As spoken in length about above, data collection methods for field research are varied. They could be a mix of surveys, interviews, case studies, and observation. All these methods have to be chalked out and the milestones for each method too have to be chalked out at the outset. For example, in the case of a survey, the survey design is important that it is created and tested even before the research begins.

Site Visit: A site visit is important to the success of the field research and it is always conducted outside of traditional locations and in the actual natural environment of the respondent/s. Hence, planning a site visit along with the methods of data collection is important.

Data Analysis: Analysis of the data that is collected is important to validate the premise of the field research and decide the outcome of the field research.

Communicating Results: Once the data is analyzed, it is important to communicate the results to the stakeholders of the research so that it could be actioned upon.

Field Research Notes

Keeping an ethnographic record is very important in conducting field research. Field notes make up one of the most important aspects of the ethnographic record. The process of field notes begins as the researcher is involved in the observational research process that is to be written down later.

Types of Field Research Notes

The four different kinds of field notes are:

Job Notes: This method of taking notes is while the researcher is in the study. This could be in close proximity and in open sight with the subject in the study. The notes here are short, concise and in a condensed form that can be built on by the researcher later. Most researchers do not prefer this method though due to the fear of feeling that the respondent may not take them seriously.

Field Notes Proper: These notes are to be expanded immediately after the completion of events. The notes have to be detailed and the words have to be as close to possible as the subject being studied.

Methodological Notes: These notes contain methods on the research methods used by the researcher, any newly proposed research methods and the way to monitor their progress. Methodological notes can be kept with field notes or filed separately but they find their way to the end report of a study.

Journals and Diaries: This method of field notes is an insight into the life of the researcher. This tracks all aspects of the researcher's life and helps eliminate the Halo effect or any bias that may have cropped up during the field research.

Reasons to Conduct Field Research

Field research has been commonly used in the 20th century in the social sciences. But in general, it takes a lot of time to conduct and complete, is expensive and in a lot of cases invasive. So why then is this commonly used and is preferred by researchers to validate data? We look at 4 major reasons:

Overcoming lack of data: Field research resolves the major issue of gaps in data. Very often, there is limited to no data about a topic in the study, especially in a specific environment. The problem might be known or suspected but there is no way to validate this without primary research and data. Conducting field research helps not only plug-in gaps in data but collect supporting material and hence is a preferred research method of researchers.

Understanding the context of the study: In many cases, the data collected is adequate but field research is still conducted. This helps gain insight into the existing data. For example, if the data states that horses from a stable farm generally win races because the horses are pedigreed and the stable owner hires the best jockeys. But conducting field research can throw light into other factors that influence the success like the quality of fodder and care provided and conducive weather conditions.

Increasing the quality of data: Since this research method uses more than one tool to collect data, the data is of higher quality. Inferences can be made from the data collected and can be statistically analyzed via the triangulation of data.

Collecting ancillary data: Field research puts the researchers in a position of localized thinking which opens them new lines of thinking. This can help collect data that the study didn't account to collect.

Examples of Field Research

Some examples of field research are:

Decipher social metrics in a slum: Purely by using observational methods and in-depth interviews, researchers can be part of a community to understand the social metrics and social hierarchy of a slum. This study can also understand the financial independence and day-to-day operational nuances of a slum. The analysis of this data can provide an insight into how different a slum is from structured societies.

Understand the impact of sports on a child's development: This method of field research takes multiple years to conduct and the sample size can be very large. The data analysis of this research provides insights into how the kids of different geographical locations and backgrounds respond to sports and the impact of sports on their all-round development.

Study animal migration patterns: Field research is used extensively to study flora and fauna. A major use case is scientists monitoring and studying animal migration patterns with the change of seasons. Field research helps collect data across years and that helps draw conclusions about how to safely expedite the safe passage of animals.

Advantages of Field Research

The advantages of field research are:

It is conducted in a real-world and natural environment where there is no tampering of variables and the environment is not doctored.

Due to the study being conducted in a comfortable environment, data can be collected even about ancillary topics.

The researcher gains a deep understanding of the research subjects due to the proximity to them and hence the research is extensive, thorough and accurate.

Disadvantages of Field Research

The disadvantages of field research are:

The studies are expensive and time-consuming and can take years to complete.

It is very difficult for the researcher to distance themselves from a bias in the research study.

The notes have to be exactly what the researcher says but the nomenclature is very tough to follow.

It is an interpretive method and this is subjective and entirely dependent on the ability of the researcher.

In this method, it is impossible to control external variables and this constantly alters the nature of the research.

TOPIC
35

CITING AND WRITING IN APA FORMAT

APA stands for the American Psychological Association.

What are the social sciences? Social sciences focus on one specific aspect of human behavior, specifically social and cultural relationships. Social sciences can include:

- Sociology
- Anthropology
- Economics
- Political Science
- Human Geography
- Archaeology
- Linguistics
- Literature
- Education

Many other fields and subject areas regularly use this style too. There are other formats and styles to use, such as MLA format and Chicago, among many, many others. If you're not sure which style to use for your research assignment or project, ask your instructor.

While writing a research paper, it is always important to give credit and cite your sources; this lets you acknowledge others' ideas and research you've used in your own work. Not doing so can be considered plagiarism, possibly leading to a failed grade or loss of a job. This style is one of the most commonly used citation styles used to prevent plagiarism. Here's more on crediting sources

A. Writing and Organizing Your Paper in an Effective Way

This section focuses on proper paper length, how to

format headings, spacing, and more!

Before getting into the details related to APA research paper format, first, determine the type of paper you're about to embark on creating:

1. Categories of papers

Empirical studies

Empirical studies take data from observations and experiments to generate research reports. It is different from other types of studies in that it isn't based on theories or ideas but on actual data.

Literature reviews

These papers analyze another individual's work or a group of works. The purpose is to gather information about a current issue or problem and to communicate where we are today. It sheds light on issues and attempts to fill those gaps with suggestions for future research and methods.

Theoretical articles

These papers are somewhat similar to literature reviews in that the author collects, examines, and shares information about a current issue or problem, by using others' research. It is different from literature reviews in that it attempts to explain or solve a problem by coming up with a new theory. This theory is justified with valid evidence.

Methodological articles

These articles showcase new advances, or modifications to an existing practice, in a scientific method or procedure. The author has data or documentation to prove that their new method, or improvement to a method, is valid. Plenty of evidence is included in this type of article. In addition, the author explains the current method being used in addition to their own findings, in order to allow the reader to understand and modify their own current practices.

Case studies

Case studies present information related to an individual, group, or larger set of individuals. These subjects are analyzed for a specific reason and the author reports on the method and conclusions from their study. The author may also make suggestions for future research, create possible theories, and/or determine a solution to a problem.

2. General paper length

Since APA style format is used often in science fields, the belief is "less is more." Make sure you're able to get your points across in a clear and brief way. Be direct, clear, and professional. Try not to add fluff and unnecessary details into your paper or writing. This will keep the paper length shorter and more concise.

3. Margin sizes

When it comes to margins, keep them consistent across the left, right, top, and bottom of the page. All four sides should be the same distance from the edge of the paper. It's recommended to use at least one-inch margins around each side. It's acceptable to use larger margins, but the margins should never be smaller than an inch.

4. Title pages

The title page, or APA format cover page, is the first page of a paper or essay. Some teachers and professors do not require a title page, but some do. If you're not sure if you should include one or not, ask your teacher. Some appreciate the page, which clearly displays the writer's name and the title of the paper.

The APA format title page includes four main components:

- The title of the APA format paper
- Running head, which includes the page number
- The author's name
- Institutional affiliation
- Some instructors and publications also ask for an author's note. If you're required or would like to include an author's note, place it below the institutional affiliation.

Here are key guidelines for developing your title page:

The title of the paper should capture the main idea of the essay, but should not contain abbreviations or words that serve no purpose. For example, instead of using the title "A Look at Amphibians From the Past," title the paper "Amphibians From the Past." Delete the unnecessary fluff!

- The title should be centered on the page and typed in 12-point, Times New Roman font. Do not underline, bold, or italicize the title.
- Your title may take up one or two lines, but should not be more than 12 words in length.
- All text on the title page should be double-spaced
- Do not include any titles in the author's name such as Dr. or Ms.
- The institutional affiliation is the school the author attends or the location where the author conducted the research.

5. Running heads

Include a page header known as the "running head" at the top of every page. To make this process easier, set your word processor to automatically add these components onto each page. You may want to look for "Header" in the features.

A running head/page header includes two pieces:

1) The title of the paper and

2) Page numbers.

Insert page numbers justified to the right-hand side of the APA format paper (do not put p. or pg. in front of the page numbers).

For the title of the paper, on the APA format title page only, include the words "Running Head" before your title in capital letters. Then type "TITLE OF YOUR PAPER" justified to the left using all capital letters. If your title is long (over 50 characters), this running head title should be a shortened version of the title of your entire paper.

6. How to form an abstract

- An APA format abstract is a summary of a scholarly article or scientific study. Scholarly articles and studies are rather lengthy documents, and abstracts allow readers to first determine if they'd like to read an article in its entirety or not.
- You may come across abstracts while researching a

topic. Many databases display abstracts in the search results and often display them before showing the full text of an article or scientific study. It is important to create a high-quality abstract that accurately communicates the purpose and goal of your paper, as readers will determine if it is worthy to continue reading or not.

- Are you wondering if you need to create an abstract for your assignment? You might not have to. Some teachers and professors require it, and others don't. If you're not sure, ask!

- If you're planning on submitting your paper to a journal for publication, first check the journal's website to learn about abstract and APA paper format requirements.

Here are some helpful suggestions to create a dynamic abstract:

- Abstracts are found on their own page, directly after the title or cover page.

- Include the running head on the top of the page.

- On the first line of the page, center the word "Abstract" (but do not include quotation marks).

- On the following line, write a summary of the key points of your research. Your abstract summary is a way to introduce readers to your research topic, the questions that will be answered, the process you took, and any findings or conclusions you drew. Use concise, brief, informative language. You only have a few sentences to share the summary of your entire document, so be direct with your wording.

- This summary should not be indented but should be double-spaced and less than 250 words.

- If applicable, help researchers find your work in databases by listing keywords from your paper after your summary. To do this, indent and type Keywords: in italics. Then list your keywords that stand out in your research. You can also include keyword strings that you think readers will type into the search box.

- Use an active voice, not a passive voice. When writing with an active voice, the subject performs the action.

When writing with a passive voice, the subject receives the action.

Active voice: The subjects reacted to the medication.

Passive voice: There was a reaction from the subjects taking the medication.

- Instead of evaluating your project in the abstract, simply report what it contains.

- If a large portion of your work includes the extension of someone else's research, share this in the abstract and include the author's last name and the year their work was released.

7. The body of most research papers

- On the page after the abstract, begin with the body of the paper. Most papers follow this format:

- Start with the Running head. The running head on the abstract page differs from the running head on the title page. The title page includes the words, "Running head." The abstract page and all other pages only show the title of the paper, in capital letters. Also include the page number. The abstract page should be page 2.

- On the next line write the title. Do not bold, underline, or italicize the title.

- Begin with the introduction and indent the first line of the paragraph.

- The introduction presents the problem and the premise upon which the research was based. It goes into more detail about this problem than the abstract.

- Begin a new section with the Method and use this word as the subtitle. Bold and center this subtitle. The Method section shows how the study was run and conducted. Be sure to describe the methods through which data was collected.

- Begin a new section with the Results. Bold and center this subtitle. The Results section summarizes your data. Use charts and graphs to display this data.

- Begin a new section with the Discussion. Bold and center this subtitle. This Discussion section is a chance to analyze and interpret your results.

- Draw conclusions and support how your data led to these conclusions.
- Discuss whether or not your hypothesis was confirmed or not supported by your results.
- Determine the limitations of the study and the next steps to improve research for future studies.

8.   Proper usage of headings & subheadings

Headings serve an important purpose in research papers — they organize your paper and make it simple to locate different pieces of information. In addition, headings provide readers with a glimpse of the main idea or content, they are about to read.

In APA format, there are five levels of headings, each with different sizes and purposes:

Level 1:
- The largest heading size
- This is the title of your paper
- The title should be centered in the middle of the page
- The title should be bolded
- Use uppercase and lowercase letters where necessary (called title capitalization)
- **Level 2:**
- Place this heading against the left margin
- Use bold letters
- Use uppercase and lowercase letters where necessary

Level 3:
- Indented in from the left side margin
- Use bold letters
- Only place an uppercase letter in the first word of the heading. All others should be lowercase. The exception is for pronouns as they should begin with a capital letter.
- End the heading with a period.

Level 4:
- Indented in from the left margin
- Bolded

- Italicized
- Only place an uppercase letter in the first word of the heading. All others should be lowercase. The exception is for pronouns as they should begin with a capital letter.
- End the heading with a period.

Level 5:

- Indented
- Italicized
- Only place an uppercase letter in the first word of the heading. All others should be lowercase. The exception is for pronouns as they should begin with a capital letter.
- End the heading with a period.

9. Use of graphics (tables and figures)

- If you're looking to enhance your project with any charts, tables, drawings, or images, there are certain APA format rules to follow.
- First and foremost, the only reason why any graphics should be added is to provide the reader with an easier way to see or read information, rather than typing it all out in the text.
- Lots of numbers to discuss? Try organizing your information into a chart or table. Pie charts, bar graphs, coordinate planes, and line graphs are just a few ways to show numerical data, relationships between numbers, and many other types of information. Instead of typing out long, drawn-out descriptions, create a drawing or image. Many visual learners would appreciate the ability to look at an image to make sense of information. Before you go ahead and place that graphic in your paper, here are a few key guidelines:
- All graphics, whether they're tables, photographs, or drawings must be numbered. The first graphic, labeled as 1, should be the first one mentioned in the text.
- Follow them in the appropriate numerical order in which they appear in the text of your paper. Example: Figure 1, Figure 2, Table 1, Figure 3.

- Only use graphics if they will supplement the material in your text. If they reinstate what you already have in your text, then it is not necessary to include a graphic.
- Include enough wording in the graphic so that the reader is able to understand its meaning, even if it is isolated from the corresponding text. However, do not go overboard with adding a ton of wording in your graphic.

Tables:

- If you have tons of numbers or data to share, consider creating a table instead of typing out a wordy paragraph. Tables are pretty easy to whip up on Google Docs or Microsoft Word.
- Here are a few pointers to keep in mind:
- Choose to type out your data OR create a table. As stated above, in APA format, you shouldn't have the information typed out in your paper and also have a table showing the same exact information. Choose one or the other.
- If you choose to create a table, discuss it very briefly in the text. Say something along the lines of, "Table 1 displays the amount of money used towards fighting Malaria." Or, "Stomach cancer rates are displayed in Table 4."
- Your table needs two items at the top:
- A number. Table 1 is the first table discussed in the paper. Table 2 is the next table mentioned, and so on.
- A title. Create a brief, descriptive title. Capitalize the first letter for each important word. Italicize the title.
- Only use horizontal lines.
- Keep the font at the 12-point size and use single or double spacing. If you use single spacing in one table, make sure all of the others use single spaces as well. Keep it consistent.
- If you need to further explain something or include an APA format citation, place it in a note below the table.
- If you're submitting your project for a class, place your table close to the text where it's mentioned. If you're submitting it to be published in a journal, most

publishers prefer tables to be placed in the back. If you're unsure where to place your tables, ask!

Figures:

- Figures represent information in a visual way. They differ from tables in that they are visually appealing. Sure, tables, like the one above, can be visually appealing, but it's the color, circles, arrows, boxes, or icons included that make a figure a "figure."
- There are many commonly used figures in papers.
- Examples APA Format:
- Pie charts
- Photographs
- Maps
- Hierarchy charts
- Drawings
- Here are some pointers to keep in mind when it comes to the APA format for figures:
- Only include a figure if it adds value to your paper. If it will truly help with understanding, include it!
- Either include a figure OR write it all out in the text. Do not include the same information twice.
- Create a sufficient caption and place it below the figure. The caption should clearly explain the content of the figure. Include any reference information if it's reproduced or adapted.

Photographs:

- We live in a world where we have tons of photographs available at our fingertips. Photographs found through Google Images, social media, stock photos made available from subscription sites, and tons of other various online sources make obtaining photographs a breeze. We can even pull out our cell phones, and in just a few seconds, take pictures with our cameras. Photographs are simple to find, and because of this, many students enjoy using them in their papers.
- If you have a photograph you would like to include in your project, here are some guidelines from the American Psychological Association.

- Create a reference for the photograph. Follow the guidelines under the "figure" section above.

- Do not use color photos. It is recommended to use black and white. Colors can change depending on the reader's screen resolution. Using black and white ensures the reader will be able to view the image clearly. The only time it is recommended to use color photos is if you're writing about color-specific things. For example, if you're discussing the various shades of leaf coloration, you may want to include a few photographs of colorful leaves.

- If there are sections of the photograph that are not related to your work, it is acceptable to crop them out. Cropping is also beneficial in that it helps the reader focus on the main item you're discussing.

- If you choose to include an image of a person you know, it would be respectful if you ask their permission before automatically including their photo in your paper. Some schools and universities post research papers online and some people prefer that their photos and information stay off the Internet.

B.   Writing Style Tips

Writing a paper for research topics is much different than writing for English, literature, and other composition classes. Science papers are much more direct, clear, and concise. This section includes key suggestions, explains how to write in APA format, and includes other pieces to keep in mind while formulating your research paper.

10. Verb usage

Research experiments and observations rely on the creation and analysis of data to test hypotheses and come to conclusions. While sharing and explaining the methods and results of studies, science writers often use verbs. When using verbs in writing, make sure that you continue to use them in the same tense throughout the section you're writing.

For verbs in scientific papers, the manual recommends using:

- Past tense or present perfect tense for the explanations of the procedure

- Past tense for the explanation of the results
- Present tense for the explanation of the conclusion and future implications

11. Proper tone

Even though your writing will not have the same fluff and detail as other forms of writing, it should not be boring or dull to read. The Publication Manual suggests thinking about who will be the main reader of your work and to write in a way that educates them.

12. Reducing bias & labels

The American Psychological Association strongly objects to any bias towards gender, racial groups, ages of individuals or subjects, disabilities, and sexual orientation. If you're unsure whether your writing is free of bias and labels or not, have a few individuals read your work to determine if it's acceptable.

Here are a few guidelines that the American Psychological Association suggests:

- Only include information about an individual's orientation or characteristic if it is important to the topic or study. Do not include information about individuals or labels if it is not necessary.

- If writing about an individual's characteristics or orientation, for essay APA format, make sure to put the person first. Instead of saying, "Diabetic patients," say, "Patients who are diabetic."

- Instead of using narrow terms such as, "adolescents," or "the elderly," try to use broader terms such as, "participants," and "subjects."

- Be mindful when using terms that end with "man" or "men" if they involve subjects who are female. For example, instead of using "Firemen," use the term, "Firefighter." In general, avoid ambiguity.

- When referring to someone's racial or ethnic identity, use the census category terms and capitalize the first letter. Also, avoid using the word, "minority," as it can be interpreted as meaning less than or deficient.

- When describing subjects in APA format, use the words "girls" and "boys" for children who are under the age of 12. The terms, "young woman," "young man," "female adolescent," and "male adolescent" are appropriate for subjects between 13-17 years old; "Men," and "women," for those older than 18. Use the term, "older adults." for individuals who are older. "Elderly," and "senior," are not acceptable if used only as nouns. It is acceptable to use these terms if they're used as adjectives.

- Read through our example essay in APA format, found in section D, to see how we've reduced bias and labels.

13. Spelling

- In APA formatting, use the same spelling as words found in Merriam-Webster's Collegiate Dictionary (American English).

- If the word you're trying to spell is not found in Webster's Collegiate Dictionary, a second resource is Webster's Third New International Dictionary.

- If attempting to properly spell words in the psychology field, consult the American Psychological Association's Dictionary of Psychology

- Thanks to helpful tools and features, such as the spell checker, in word processing programs, most of us think we have everything we need right in our document.

14. Abbreviation do's and don'ts

- Abbreviations can be tricky. You may be asking yourself, "Do I include periods between the letters?" "Are all letters capitalized?" "Do I need to write out the full name each and every time?" Not to worry, we're breaking down abbreviations for you here. First and foremost, use abbreviations sparingly. Too many and you're left with a paper littered with capital letters mashed together. Plus, they don't lend themselves to smooth and easy reading. Readers need to pause and comprehend the meaning of abbreviations and quite often stumble over them.

- If the abbreviation is used less than three times in the paper, type it out each time. It would be pretty difficult to remember what an abbreviation or acronym stands for if you're writing a lengthy paper.

- If you decide to sprinkle in abbreviations, it is not necessary to include periods between the letters.
- Prior to using an unfamiliar abbreviation, you must type it out in text and place the abbreviation immediately following it in parentheses. Any usage of the abbreviation after the initial description can be used without the description.
- Example: While it may not affect a patient's short-term memory (STM), it may affect their ability to comprehend new terms. Patients who experience STM loss while using the medication should discuss it with their doctor.
- If an abbreviation is featured in Merriam-Webster's Collegiate Dictionary as is, then it is not necessary to spell it out.
- Example: AIDS
- For units of measurement, include the abbreviation if it sits with a number. If the unit of measurement stands alone, type it out.
- Examples APA format:
- 4 lbs.
- The weight in pounds exceeded what we previously thought.

15. Spacing

The manual recommends using one space after most punctuation marks unless the punctuation mark is at the end of a sentence. If the punctuation mark is at the end of the sentence, use two spaces afterward. Yes, we know this seems a bit outdated. It doesn't hurt to double-check with your teacher or professor to ask their preference. The official APA format book was primarily created to aid individuals with submitting their research paper for publication in a professional journal. Many schools adopt certain parts of the handbook and modify sections to match their preference.

16. Other word rules

It's often a heated debate among writers whether or not to use an Oxford comma, but for this style, always use an Oxford comma. This type of comma is placed before the words AND and OR or in a series of three items.

Example of APA format for commas:

The medication caused drowsiness, upset stomach, and fatigue.

Here's another example:

The subjects chose between cold, room temperature, or warm water.

When writing a possessive singular noun, you should place the apostrophe before the s. For possessive plural nouns, the apostrophe is placed after the s.

Singular: Linda Morris's jacket

Plural: The Morris' house

For hyphens, do not place a space before or after the hyphen. Here's an example:

custom-built

17. Number rules

Science papers often include the use of numbers, usually displayed in data, tables, and experiment information. The golden rule to keep in mind is that numbers less than 10 are written out in the text. If the number is more than 10, use numerals.

APA format examples:

- 14 kilograms
- seven individuals
- 83 years old
- Fourth grade
- The golden rule for numbers has exceptions.
- In APA formatting, use numerals if you are:
- Showing numbers in a table or graph
- Referring to information in a table or graph

Table 7

Including a unit of measurement directly after it. Examples APA format:

- 8 lbs.
- 5 cm

- Displaying a math equation
- 4 divided by 2
- Showing a time, age, or date
- 8:08 a.m.
- 6-month-olds

Use numbers which are written out as words if you are:

- Starting the sentence with a number (but try to rearrange the sentence to avoid this!)
- Ninety-two percent of teachers feel as though....
- Writing out a commonly used word or saying
- Hundred Years' War
- Including a fraction
- One-sixth of the students
- Showing a time, age, or date
- 8:08 a.m.
- 6-month-olds

Other APA formatting number rules to keep in mind:

- Always include a zero before a decimal point
  0.13 g
- Keep Roman numerals as is. Do not translate them into Arabic numerals. Examples APA format:
- World War II
- Super Bowl LII
- If you're including plurals, do not include an apostrophe!
- It's the 1980s, not the 1980's!

C.   Brief Overviews

18. Overview of references

- An APA format reference and an APA format citation are two different things! We understand that many teachers and professors use the terms as if they're synonyms, but according to this specific style, they are two separate things, with different purposes, and styled differently.

- A reference displays all of the information about the source — the title, the author's name, the year it was published, the URL, all of it! References are placed on the final page of a research project. Here's an example of a reference:

- Wynne-Jones, T. (2015). The emperor of any place. Somerville: MA, Candlewick Press.

- An APA format citation is an APA format in-text citation. These are found within your paper, anytime a quote or paraphrase is included. They usually only include the name of the author and the date the source was published. Here's an example of one:

- Hypertrophic cardiomyopathy is even discussed in the book, The Emperor of Any Place. The main character, Evan, finds a mysterious diary on his father's desk (the same desk his father died on, after suffering from a hypertrophic cardiomyopathy attack). Evan unlocks the truth to his father and grandfather's past (Wynne-Jones 2015).

- Both of the ways to credit another individual's work — in the text of a paper and also on the final page — are key to preventing plagiarism. A writer must use both types in a paper. If you cite something in the text, it must have a full reference on the final page of the project. Where there is one, there must be the other!

- Now that you understand that, here's some basic info regarding APA format references.

- Each reference is organized, or structured, differently. It all depends on the source type. A book reference is structured one way, an APA journal is structured a different way, a newspaper article is another way. Yes, it's probably frustrating that not all references are created equal and set up the same way. MLA works cited pages are unique in that every source type is formatted the same way. Unfortunately, this style is quite different.

Most references follow this general format:

- Author's Last name, First initial. Middle initial. (Year published). Title of source. URL.

- Again, as stated in the above paragraph, you must

look up the specific source type you're using to find out the placement of the title, author's name, year published, etc.

19. In-text citations

Did you find the perfect quote or piece of information to include in your project? Way to go! It's always a nice feeling when we find that magical piece of data or info to include in our writing. You probably already know that you can't just copy and paste it into your project, or type it in, without also providing credit to the original author.

Displaying where the original information came from is much easier than you think. Directly next to the quote or information you included, place the author's name and the year nearby. This allows the reader of your work to see where the information originated.

Here are two APA format citation examples:

Harlem had many artists and musicians in the late 1920s (Belafonte, 2008).

Or, you can place the author's name in the sentence itself.

According to Belafonte (2008), Harlem was full of artists and musicians in the late 1920s.

The author's names are structured differently if there is more than one author. Things will also look different if there isn't an author at all (which is sometimes the case with website pages). For more information on APA citation format, check out this page on the topic: APA parenthetical citation and APA in-text citation.

20. References page

An APA format reference page is easier to create than you probably think. We go into detail on how to create this page on our APA Works Cited page. If you're simply looking for a brief overview of the reference page, we've got you covered here.

Here are some pointers to keep in mind when it comes to the references page in APA format:

- This VIP page has its very own page. Start on a fresh, clean document.
- Begin with the running head at the top, as always.
- Center and bold the title "References" (do not include quotation marks, underline, or italicize this title).

- Alphabetize and double-space ALL entries.
- Use Times New Roman, 12-pt size.
- Every quote or piece of outside information included in the paper should be referenced and have an entry.
- Even though it's called a "reference page," it can be longer than one page. If your references flow onto the next page, then that's a-okay.

E. Final Checklist

- Prior to submitting your paper, check to make sure you have everything you need and everything in its place:
- Did you credit all of the information and quotes you used in the body of your paper and show a matching full reference at the end of the paper? Remember, you need both! Did you include a running head on every single page of your project? Are page numbers included? Only include the words "Running head" on the title page.
- Is your title page properly formatted? You may feel tempted to make the title in a larger font size or add graphics to jazz it up a bit. Keep it professional looking and make everything 12 pt size font and double spaced.
- If you created an abstract, is it directly after the title page? Some teachers and professors do not require an abstract, so before you go ahead and include it, make sure it's something he or she is expecting.
- Are all headings, as in section or chapter titles, properly formatted? If you're not sure, check section number 9.
- Are all tables and figures aligned properly? Did you include notes and other important information directly below the image? Include any information that will help the reader completely understand everything in the table or figure if it were to stand alone.
- Are abbreviations used sparingly? Did you format them properly?
- Is the entire document double spaced?
- Are all numbers formatted properly? Check section 17,

which is the APA writing format for numbers.

- Did you glance at the sample paper? Is your assignment structured similarly? Are all of the margins uniform?

F. Submitting Your Paper

If you're planning to submit your paper as an assignment, make sure you review your teacher's or professor's procedures. If you're submitting your paper to a journal, you probably need to include a cover letter. **Most cover letters ask you to include:**

- The author's contact information.
- A statement to the editor that the paper is original.
- If a similar paper exists elsewhere, notify the editor in the cover letter.
- Once again, review the specific journal's website for exact specifications for submission.

Further Information on the Style

This citation style was created by the American Psychological Association. Its rules and guidelines can be found in the Publication Manual of the American Psychological Association. The information provided above follows the 6th edition (2009) of the manual. The 7th edition was published in 2019 and is the most recent version.

What's New in the 7th Edition?

- The 7th edition of the Publication Manual is in full color and includes 12 sections (compared to 8 sections in the 6th edition). In general, this new edition differentiates between professional and student papers, includes guidance with accessibility in mind, provides new examples to follow, and has updated guidelines.
- Cover page. For student papers, the cover page should include all of the following details:
- Paper title
- Student name
- Affiliation (e.g., school, department, etc.)
- Course number and title

- Course instructor
- Due date
- Font. Recommended fonts include:
- 12-pt. Times New Roman
- 11-pt. Calibri, Arial, Georgia
- 10-pt. Lucida, Sans Unicode, Computer Modern
- Running heads. These are no longer required for student papers. When included in professional papers, do not include the words "Running head:" before the paper title/head. For example:
- 6th edition – Running head: SMARTPHONE EFFECTS ON ADOLESCENT SOCIALIZATION
- 7th edition – SMARTPHONE EFFECTS ON ADOLESCENT SOCIALIZATION
- Pronouns. "They" can be used as a gender-neutral pronoun.
- Bias-free language guidelines. There are updated and new sections on guidelines for this section. New sections address participation in research, socioeconomic status, and intersectionality.
- Spacing after sentences. Add only a single space after the end punctuation.
- Tables and figures. The citing format is now streamlined so that both tables and figures should include a name and number above the table/figure and a note underneath the table/figure.
- In-text citations. If there are 3 or more source authors, you can shorten the reference by using "eg al." after the first name.
- 6th ed. – (Ikemoto, Richardson, Murphy, Yoshida 2016)
- 7th ed. – (Ikemoto et al., 2016)
- Citing books. The location of the publisher can be omitted.
- Using DOIs. DOI numbers should be formatted as a URL.
- Example: https://doi.org/10.1038/s42255-019-0153-5
- Using URLs. URLs no longer need to be prefaced by the words "Retrieved from."

TOPIC

36

CITING AND WRITING
IN MLA FORMAT

The Modern Language Association (MLA) is an organization responsible for developing MLA format, often called MLA style. MLA format was developed as a means for researchers, students, and scholars in the literature and language fields to use a uniform way to format their papers and assignments. This uniform or consistent, method of developing an MLA paper or assignment allows for easy reading. Today, MLA is not only used in literature and language subject areas; many others have adopted it as well.

The Modern Language Association released the 8th and most current edition of their Handbook in April 2016. The Handbook provides thorough instructions on MLA format citing, as well as guidelines for submitting work that adheres to the Modern Language Association's rules and standards. Although we're not affiliated with the MLA, our citation specialists bring you this thoughtful and informative guide on the format.

1.   Paper Choice

- If you choose to print your MLA format paper, use white paper only. Do not use ivory, off-white, or any other shades or colors.

- Choose a standard, high-quality paper to print your project on. Do not use cardstock. It is not necessary to use resume paper. Use typical, high-quality printer or copy paper.

- When it comes to size, 8 ½-by-11-inch paper is the recommended size. If you'd like to use a different size, ask your teacher prior to submission.

2.   MLA Heading Instructions

There are two options when it comes to creating the MLA header for your project:

An MLA format heading can be placed at the top of the first page, or,

A title page can grace the front of the assignment. If you choose to create a title page, keep in mind that there aren't any official MLA title page or MLA format cover page guidelines. See more information below.

- If choosing option 1, creating an MLA heading, you'll need to include four main components:
- Your full name
- Your instructor's name
- The name of the course or class
- The assignment's due date
- The first item typed on the MLA format paper should be your full name. Position your name one inch from the top and left margins of the page. Add a double space beneath your name, and type the name of your instructor. Below the professor, or instructor's name, should be a double space, followed by the name of the course, class, or section number (if available). Below it, include another double space and add the assignment's due date.
- The assignment's title should be placed below the due date, after a double space. Align the title so it sits in the center of the MLA format paper. The title should be written in standard lettering, without underlines, bold font, italicized font, or any quotation marks. Only include italics if your title includes the title of another source.
- Here is an example of an MLA header for an MLA format essay, paper, or assignment:
- Neal ....
- Professor ....
- English 201
- 2 Nov 2020
- Most research papers use a standard MLA format

heading, like the one seen above. If your instructor requires you to create a standalone title page, ask him or her for specifications. MLA does not have specific instructions for developing an MLA title page. We recommend you use an MLA header for your project.

- If your teacher or professor requires a standalone title page but has not provided any guidance or specifications, here are a few suggestions

- Place the title of the assignment in the center of the page. Do not bold the title, italicize the entire title, place quotation marks around it, or type the title out in capital letters.

- Use italics for the titles of any sources in the title of your paper. Example: An Analysis of Mythical Creatures in the Harry Potter Series

- The title should be written in title case form. Capitalize the:

- the first letter of the title

- first letter of the last word

- first letter of any adjectives, adverbs, nouns, pronouns, and verbs

- Add the same information from the header (your name, the name of your instructor, the name of the course or class, and the assignment's due date) and center the information in the middle of the paper below the title.

- Double-space the entire page.

- Keep the font size at 12 pt., or a size close to it, to make it look professional.

- Use the same font as the text of the paper. The Modern Language Association recommends any font that is easy to read and has a clear distinction between italics and standard font. Times New Roman and Arial are recommended, but many other fonts work as well.

- Include a page number in the top right corner of the paper. For more information on how to style page numbers, check out the next section, "Running Head and Page Numbers."

- We do not recommend adding any images or cover art to the title page.

3. Running Head & Page Numbers

- A running head is a brief heading that is placed in the top right corner of every page in a project. The running head consists of the writer's last name, followed by a space, and then the page number.
- Here is an example of a running head that might be seen in the top right corner of a research paper:
- Altaf 7
- The running head is placed half an inch from the top margin and one inch from the right margin of the page.
- Do not place the word "page," or use an abbreviation, such as p. or pg., before the page number.
- General tips to keep in mind:
- Placed in the upper right-hand corner, one-half inch from the top, flush with the right margin.
- Type your last name before the page number. (To make this process easier, set your word processor to automatically add the last name and page number to each page).
- Do not place p. before the page number.
- Many instructors do not want a page number on the first page. Ask your instructor for their specific preferences.
- Before adding this information manually onto every single page, check to see if the word processor you're using has the capability to automatically add this information for you. Try looking in the settings area where page numbers or headers can be added or modified.
- Quite often, the running head and page numbers begin on the second page, but your instructor may ask you to include the running head on the first page of the assignment. As always, if your instructor provides you with specific directions, follow his or her guidelines.

4. Margins

- Use one-inch margins around the entire page. The running head should be the only item seen in the one-inch margin

- Most word processing programs automatically default to using one-inch margins. Check the page settings section of the program to locate the margin size.

5. Paragraphs

- Indent the first word in every paragraph. Sentences should begin one-half inch from the left margin.

- It is not necessary to manually measure half an inch. Use the "tab" button on the keyboard to create a half-inch space.

- Like all other sections of the assignment, paragraphs should be double spaced.

6. Quotations

- Quotes are added into assignments to help defend an argument, prove a point, add emphasis, or simply liven up a project.

- Quotes should not take up the majority of your paper or assignment. Quotes should be sprinkled sparingly throughout. Use direct quotes from outside sources to enhance and expand on your own writing and ideas.

- Words from quotes belong to the individual who spoke or wrote them, so it is essential to credit that individual's work. Credit him or her by adding what is called an "MLA format in-text citation" into the body of the project.

- There are three ways to add quotes:

- With the person's name in the sentence.

- Example:

- Dan Gutman shares a glimpse into the overall plot by stating, "I didn't know it at the time, but a baseball card—for me—could function like a time machine" (5).

- In the above example, Dan Gutman is the author of the book that this quote is pulled from.

- Without the person's name in the sentence

- Example:

- The main character's confusing experience is realized and explained when he states "I didn't know it at the time, but a baseball card—for me—could function like a time machine" (Gutman 5).

- In the above example, Dan Gutman's name isn't included in the sentence. It's included in the parentheses at the end of the sentence. This is an example of a proper MLA style citation in the body of a project.

- In a block quote, which is used when a large quote, of 4 lines or more, is added into a project.

- Using footnotes and endnotes:

- The Modern Language Association generally promotes the use of references as described in the sections above, but footnotes and endnotes are also acceptable forms of references to use in your paper.

- Footnotes and endnotes are helpful to use in a variety of circumstances. Here are a few scenarios when it may seem appropriate to use this type of reference:

- When you are referring to a number of various sources, by various authors, in a section of your paper. In this situation, it is a good idea to use a footnote or endnote to share information for parenthetical references. This will encourage the reader to stay focused on the text of the research paper, instead of having to read through all of the reference information.

- When you are sharing additional information that doesn't quite fit into the scope of the paper but is beneficial for the reader. These types of footnotes and endnotes are helpful when explaining translations, adding background information, or sharing counterexamples to research.

- To include a footnote or endnote, add a superscript number at the end of the sentence the footnote or endnote refers to. They can be included mid-sentence if necessary, but be sure to add it after any punctuation, such as commas or periods. Find a location that doesn't distract the reader from the content and flow of the paper.

- Here's an example:
- Within the text:
- Numerous well-known children's books include characters from a wide range of races and ethnicities, thus promoting diversity and multiculturalism.[1]
- At the bottom of the page (footnote) or at the end of the section (endnote)

7. Paraphrases

- Paraphrases are created when text or speech from another source are added into a project, but the writer chooses to summarize them and weave in his or her own writing and writing style.

- Even though the writer modifies the information from another source, it is still necessary to credit the source using proper MLA format. Paraphrased information uses the same MLA reference format as stated in the section directly above this one.

- Here is an acceptable paraphrase:

Original text:

> "Stay hungry. Stay foolish." Steve Jobs

Paraphrase

Steve Jobs encouraged students at Stanford to continue with their determination, drive, and ambitious behavior. They should never be simply satisfied with the status quo. They should continue to push themselves despite possible obstacles and failures.

- To develop a well-written paraphrase, follow these simple, step-by-step instructions.

- Find a phrase, sentence, paragraph, or section of original text you'd like to turn into a paraphrase.

- Read the text carefully and make sure you fully comprehend its meaning. A writer can only develop a well-written paraphrase if the information has been fully grasped and understood. If you're having difficulty understanding the information, take a few minutes to read up on tricky words and background information. If all else fails, ask a friend to see if they're able to make sense of the concepts.

- After analyzing and completely understanding the original text, put it to the side. Take a moment to think about what you've read and connected the idea to your own assignment.

- Now that the information is completely understood, take a moment to rewrite what you've read, in your own words and writing style. Do not simply substitute words in the original text with synonyms. That's plagiarism! Show off and demonstrate your ability to process the original information, connect it to the content in your paper, and write it in your own individual and unique writing style.

- Include an in-text reference next to the paraphrase. All paraphrases include references, similar to direct quotes. See section 6 of this guide to learn how to properly attribute your paraphrased information.

- Give yourself a pat on the back! Paraphrasing is an important part of the research and writing process.

- Wondering if it's better to quote or paraphrase?

- An essential part of the research process involves adding direct quotes and paraphrases into projects. Direct quotes provide word-for-word evidence and allow writers to use another author's eloquent words and language in their own projects. When it comes to paraphrases, writers are able to take a block of text and shrink the scope of it into their papers. Paper writers can also use paraphrases to demonstrate their ability to analyze and reiterate information in a meaningful and relevant way.

- If you're wondering which one is better to consistently use, quotes or paraphrases, there's a clear winner. Paraphrases come out on top. Sure, direct quotes are incredibly beneficial, but copying and pasting too many of these into a project can cause a reader to lose sight of the writer's own voice. Mixing your own voice with another author's too much can make for choppy and disjointed reading.

- The ultimate goal of a research project is to have your voice and research merged together as one. Paraphrases allow just that. When you combine information from outside sources with your own writing style, it demonstrates your ability as a researcher to showcase your understanding and analysis of a topic.

- Remember, whether you're adding direct quotes or paraphrases into a project, both types of additions need references. References are placed after the quotes and paraphrases, and also at the end of an assignment.

8. Spacing

- MLA research paper format requires that the entire research paper or MLA format essay includes double-spaced lines. Double-spaced lines should be found in between the written body of the work, in the heading, and also on the MLA reference page.

- While it may seem tempting to place a few extra lines between the heading, title, and beginning of the paper, lines should all be double spaced.

9.   Font and Font Size

- In an MLA paper, it is acceptable to use any font type that is easy to read. Many source types, such as books and articles, use fonts that are easy to read, so if you're seeking an appropriate font style, look at other sources for guidance. Two of the most commonly used fonts are Arial and Times New Roman.

- It is important for the reader to be able to distinguish the difference between italicized and regular font, so if you choose a font style different than Arial or Times New Roman, make sure the difference between the two type styles is evident.

- The use of 12-point font size is recommended as this is the default size for many word processing programs. It is acceptable to use another standard size, such as 11-point or 11.5-point.

General guidelines:

- Use white 8 ½ x 11" paper.
- Make 1-inch margins on the top, bottom, and sides
- The first word in every paragraph should be indented one-half inch.
- Indent set-off quotations one inch from the left margin

- Use any type of font that is easy to read, such as Times New Roman. Make sure that italics look different from the regular typeface.
- Use 12 point size
- Double-space the entire research paper, even the works cited page.
- Leave one space after periods and other punctuation marks, unless your instructor tells you to make two spaces.
- To create a header, follow these steps:
- Begin one inch from the top of the first page and flush with the left margin.
- Type your name, your instructor's name, the course number, and the date on separate lines, using double spaces between each.
- Double-space once more and center the title. Do NOT underline, bold, or type the title in all capital letters. Only italicize words that would normally be italicized in the text. Example: Character Development in The Great Gatsby
- Do not place a period after the title or after any headings
- Double-space between the title and first lines of the text

10. Punctuation

- Here are a few guidelines to keep in mind in relation to punctuation marks.
- Commas: Use commas when it makes sense for individuals to pause while reading or to help with understanding.
- Concluding Sentences: When closing out a sentence with the use of a punctuation mark, begin the following sentence after one space, not two spaces.
- Quotes: When including a quote in your paper or assignment, place the period outside of the parentheses, at the end of the entire sentence.
- Here is an example of MLA format:
- "One good thing about music, when it hits you feel no

pain" (Marley).

- Notice that the period is on the outside of the parentheses, not at the end of the quote itself.

11. Abbreviations

Abbreviations are commonly used in many source types including websites, blog posts, books, and journal articles. It is acceptable to use abbreviations in all of these sources. When it comes to school and research assignments however, the Modern Language Association prefers abbreviations to rarely be used. Spelling out abbreviations into their full words and meaning is recommended. This ensures understanding and avoids any confusion. Instead of coming across choppy abbreviations, readers can follow the natural flow of the language in the paper.

There are times when you may feel it is perfectly acceptable to use an abbreviation rather than its typed out counterpart in a paper.

When including abbreviations, do not place periods in between capital letters.

Examples:

- Human Immunodeficiency Virus can be abbreviated to HIV, not H.I.V.
- United States should be US, not U.S.
- Digital video disc should be DVD, not D.V.D.
- For lower case abbreviations, it is acceptable to include periods between the letters.
- The abbreviation, "For example" = e.g.
- If there is a mix of lower case and upper case letters, do not use periods if the majority of the letters are upper case.

Examples:

- PhD
- EdD
- Months
- Type out entire month names when being used in the body of a research paper or assignment. Example:
- She rented out the beach house from May through September.

- When it comes to references, MLA bibliography format requires months longer than four letters to be abbreviated.

MLA Format Example:

- July = July
- November = Nov.
- Other abbreviations that are perfectly acceptable to use in a bibliography in MLA format (not the body of a project) include:
- or pp. for page and page numbers
- ch. for chapter
- ed. for edition
- trans. for translation or translated
- vol. for volume
- no. for number
- rev. for revised

Again, these abbreviations should only be used on the final page of a project, the MLA reference page. They should not be used in the body of a project.

Publishers

One of the quirkiest things about this particular style is how publisher names are structured on the final page of references. Certain words are abbreviated and other words are written in full.

Here's a breakdown of the words that are always abbreviated on the final page's references:

- U = University
- Co. = Company
- Inc. = Incorporated
- Ltd. = Limited
- P = Press
- Here are a few examples:
- U of Delaware
- Constable and Co. Ltd.
- Pimlico Books at Random House
- U College of London P

All other words related to the names of publishers should be written out in full

Titles

Certain classical and biblical works are abbreviated on the final page of references, but also in any references in the text that are in parentheses.

The official handbook provides a lengthy list, spanning over multiple pages, of the preferred abbreviations to use for classical and biblical works, but here's a quick snapshot of some of the commonly used ones:

- Hebrew Bible or Old Testament = OT
- Deut. = Deuteronomy
- Gen. = Genesis
- Lev. = Leviticus
- Num. = Numbers
- Ps. = Psalms
- New Testament = NT
- 1 Cor. = 1 Corinthians
- Jas. = James
- Matt. = Matthew
- Shakespeare:
- Ado = Much Ado about Nothing
- 3H6 = Henry VI, Part 3
- JC = Julius Caesar
- Mac. = Macbeth
- MND = Midsummer Night's Dream
- Oth. = Othello
- Rom. = Romeo and Juliet

Again, the titles above are allowed to be abbreviated both in references in parentheses in the body of a project and also on the final page of references. If you're wondering why it's because they're cited often and it's unnecessary to type out the entire title names.

12. Numbers

Use of Numerals

If the project calls for frequent use of numbers (such

as a scientific study or statistics), use numerals that precede measurements.

Example:

- 247 milligrams
- 5 pounds
- Other items to keep in mind:
- In divisions, use numbers, ex: In page 5 of the study

In the next section, you'll find instructions for using Arabic and Roman numerals in a project.

Arabic Numbers

When including a number in a paper, spell out the number if it can be written as one word (such as six) or two words (such as sixty-two). For fractions, decimals, or longer numbers, type them out using digits. For larger numbers, write the number itself.

Here are a few examples:

- one
- 2 ½
- three
- 8 ½
- 17.953
- eighteen
- twenty-seven
- forty-four
- one hundred
- 101
- 247
- 5,306

If the number comes before a unit of measurement or label, type the number using digits.

- 4 pounds
- 8 tablespoons
- 3 years
- 9 chapters
- 3 July 2018
- 25 King Street

- 5 a.m.
- 5 o'clock

More on Numbers

- Starting a sentence with a number is generally frowned upon. Try modifying the sentence so that the number, or number word, is found elsewhere.
- Instead of:
- 225 children were found in the warehouse, some malnourished and diseased.
- Use the sentence:
- A total of 225 children were found in the warehouse, some malnourished and diseased.
- If modifying the sentence is not possible or does not work well with the flow of the assignment or paper, type out the written number:
- Two hundred twenty-five children were found in the warehouse, some malnourished and diseased.
- Do not include any ISBN numbers in your paper.

13. Images, Tables, & Musical Scores

Photographs, data sets, tables, graphs, and other images are often added into projects or papers to promote or aid understanding. They provide meaningful visuals for the reader. If the illustration or visual image does not enhance the quality of the paper, do not include it in the project.

- Tables and illustrations should be placed as close as possible to the text that they most closely refer to.
- Images
- For an image to be significant and easily identifiable, place it as close as possible to the text in the project where it is discussed.
- It is not acceptable to simply place an image in a project without including identifiable information. All images must include information about their origin.
- Here are the directions to properly attribute an image:
- Create a label for the image or illustration and place it directly beneath the image. Begin the label with the abbreviation "Fig.," which is short for a figure.

- Assign an Arabic number. The image closest to the beginning of the project should be labeled as Fig. 1. The next image in the project should be Fig. 2. and so on.
- Provide a caption. The label and caption should appear underneath the illustration.
- *If the table or illustration's caption gives complete information about the source and the source isn't cited in the text, there is no need to include the citation in the works cited page.

In the text of the project or paper, place a parenthesis at the end of the line where the figure is discussed, and include the label.

Example:

Sarah's tattoo design was filled with two of her favorite flowers; lilies and daffodils along a thinly curved vine (fig. 1).

Create a caption for the image. The caption should be a brief explanation or title of the contents of the image. Place the caption directly next to the label.

Immediately following the caption, it is acceptable to include attribution information. If the image is not discussed further in the rest of the paper or project, it is acceptable to include the MLA bibliography format citation below the image and omitted from the bibliography or MLA format works cited page.

Tables

When adding a table or data set into a project, do not place the label "fig." below the information. Instead, above the data set, including the label, "Table." Label tables with "Table," give it an Arabic numeral, and title it. This information should be located above the table, flush left, on separate lines.

- The table's title should be written in title case form (the first letter of each word is capitalized, except for small, insignificant words).
- Underneath the table, provide the source and any notes. Notes should be labeled with a letter, rather than a numeral, so the reader is able to differentiate between the notes of the text and the notes of the

table.

- Use double spacing throughout.
- In MLA format, the first table seen in the project is labeled as Table 1. The second table in the project is Table 2, and so on.

14. Lists

- It's appropriate to add lists into an MLA format essay as long as the proper rules are followed.
- Lists created using MLA essay format look different than a grocery list or any other type of vertical listing of items. Items in a list are formatted in horizontal order, rather than the traditional vertical style.
- Here is an example of how a list may look in a research project or assignment:
- William Shakespeare wrote numerous plays, many of which were considered tragedies: Romeo & Juliet, Hamlet, Macbeth, Othello, Julius Caesar, and King Lear.
- Notice the items are listed horizontally, not vertically. This is important to keep in mind when including lists in a project.
- Place a colon between the introductory sentence and the list. There are also times when a colon is not included. Do not place a colon before the first list item if the list is part of the sentence.
- Here is an example of how a list may look in a research project or assignment when the list is part of the sentence.
- Many of William Shakespeare's were tragedies. Some of his most popular tragedies include Romeo & Juliet, Hamlet, Macbeth, Othello, Julius Caesar, and King Lear.

15. Works Cited MLA Format

Here are a few items to keep in mind when developing this portion of a project:

- The list of citations should be the very last page of a research project or essay
- The top of the page should include the running head

and the final page number
* All entries should be placed in alphabetical order by the first item in the MLA format citation
* The entire page should be double spaced

16. MLA Format Citing

The majority of this guide focuses on MLA formatting in regards to MLA paper format rules and guidelines.

Here's the proper order:

* Author's Last name, Author's First name. "Title of Source." Title of Container, Names of other contributors along with their specific roles, Version of the source (if it differs from the original or is unique), Any key numbers associated with the source that aren't dates (such as journal issue numbers or volume numbers), Name of the Publisher, Publication date, Location (such as the location of specific page numbers or a website's address).

17. Binding

* Some professors or instructors will provide guidance on how to secure hard copies of projects. If your instructor does not provide you with any expectations or guidance, a simple staple in the top left corner should suffice. If a stapler is not available, some instructors allow paper or binder clips.
* Do not fold the top left corner down to secure the pages together. The page could easily unfold, causing a mess of papers. While binders and plastic holders are cute, in reality, they add bulk to a professor or instructor who may like to take the papers home for grading purposes. Keep the binding simple and clean. Staples work best, and binder and paper clips are the next best option.
* As always, follow any instructions your professor or teacher may provide. The guidelines found here are simply recommendations.

18. Edits and Proofreading

Editing and proofreading your assignment prior to submission is an incredibly important step in the research process. Editing involves checking the paper for the following items:

Spelling: Are all words spelled correctly? Review all proper names, places, and other unique words to ensure correct spelling. When finished, run the project through a spell checker. Many word processing programs, such as Microsoft Word and Google Drive, provide a free spell-checking feature. While spell checks are beneficial, they do not always spot every mistake, so make sure you take the time to read through the assignment carefully. If you're still not sure if your project contains proper spelling, ask a friend to read through it. They may find a mistake you missed!

Grammar: Check your assignment to make sure you've included proper word usage. There are numerous grammar checkers available to review your project prior to submission. Again, take the time to review any recommendations from these programs prior to accepting the suggestions and revisions.

Punctuation: Check to make sure the end of every sentence has an ending punctuation mark. Also make sure commas, hyphens, colons, and other punctuation marks are placed in the appropriate places.

Attribution: Do all quotes and paraphrases include an MLA format citation? Did you create an in-text citation for each individual piece of information?

19. Submission

Follow your instructor's guidelines for submitting your assignment. Your instructor may ask you to submit a hard copy or submit it electronically via email or through a course management system.

TOPIC
37

RESEARCH METHODS KEY TERM
GLOSSARY

Aim

The researcher's area of interest – what they are looking at (e.g. to investigate helping behavior).

Bar chart

A graph that shows the data in the form of categories (e.g. behaviors observed) that the researcher wishes to compare.

Behavioral categories

Key behaviors or, collections of behavior, that the researcher conducting the observation will pay attention to and record

Case study

In-depth investigation of a single person, group or event, where data are gathered from a variety of sources and by using several different methods (e.g. observations & interviews).

Closed questions

Questions where there are fixed choices of responses e.g. yes/no. They generate quantitative data

Co-variables

The variables investigated in a correlation

Concurrent validity

Comparing a new test with another test of the same thing to see if they produce similar results. If they do then the new test has concurrent validity

Confidentiality

Unless agreed beforehand, participants have the right to expect that all data collected during a research study will remain confidential and anonymous.

Confounding variable

An extraneous variable that varies systematically with the IV so we cannot be sure of the true source of the change to the DV

Content analysis

A technique used to analyze qualitative data which involves coding the written data into categories – converting qualitative data into quantitative data.

Control group

A group that is treated normally and gives us a measure of how people behave when they are not exposed to the experimental treatment (e.g. allowed to sleep normally).

Controlled observation

An observation study where the researchers control some variables - often takes place in a laboratory setting

Correlational analysis

A mathematical technique where the researcher looks to see whether scores for two covariables are related

Counterbalancing

A way of trying to control for order effects in a repeated measures design, e.g. half the participants do condition A followed by B and the other half do B followed by A

Covert observation

Also known as an undisclosed observation as the participants do not know their behavior is being observed

Critical value

The value that a test statistic must reach in order for the hypothesis to be accepted.

Debriefing

After completing the research, the true aim is revealed to the participant. Aim of debriefing = to return the person to the state s/he was in before they took part.

Deception

Involves misleading participants about the purpose of s study.

Demand characteristics

Occur when participants try to make sense of the research situation they are in and try to guess the purpose of the research or try to present themselves in a good way.

Dependent variable

The variable that is measured to tell you the outcome.

Descriptive statistics

Analysis of data that helps describe, show or summarize data in a meaningful way

Directional hypothesis

A one-tailed hypothesis that states the direction of the difference or relationship (e.g. boys are more helpful than girls).

Dispersion measure

A dispersion measure shows how a set of data is spread out, examples are the range and the standard deviation

Double-blind control

Participants are not told the true purpose of the research and the experimenter is also blind to at least some aspects of the research design.

Ecological validity

The extent to which the findings of a research study are able to be generalized to real-life settings

Ethical guidelines

These are provided by the BPS - they are the 'rules' by which all psychologists should operate, including those carrying out research.

Ethical issues

There are 3 main ethical issues that occur in psychological research – deception, lack of informed consent and lack of protection of participants.

Evaluation apprehension

Participants' behavior is distorted as they fear being judged by observers

Event sampling

A target behavior is identified and the observer records it every time it occurs

Experimental group

The group that received the experimental treatment (e.g. sleep deprivation)

External validity

Whether it is possible to generalize the results beyond the experimental setting.

Extraneous variable

Variables that if not controlled may affect the DV and provide a false impression than an IV has produced changes when it hasn't.

Face validity

A simple way of assessing whether a test measures what it claims to measure which is concerned with face value – e.g. does an IQ test look like it tests intelligence.

Field experiment

An experiment that takes place in a natural setting where the experimenter manipulates the IV and measures the DV

Histogram

A graph that is used for continuous data (e.g. test scores). There should be no space between the bars because the data is continuous.

Hypothesis

This is a formal statement or prediction of what the researcher expects to find. It needs to be testable.

Independent groups design

An experimental design where each participant only takes part in one condition of the IV

Independent variable

The variable that the experimenter manipulates (changes).

Inferential statistics

Inferential statistics are ways of analyzing data using statistical tests that allow the researcher to make conclusions about whether a hypothesis was supported by the results.

Informed consent

Psychologists should ensure that all participants are helped to understand fully all aspects of the research before they agree (give consent) to take part

Inter-observer reliability

The extent to which two or more observers are observing and recording behavior in the same way

Internal validity

In relation to experiments, whether the results were due to the manipulation of the IV rather than other factors such as extraneous variables or demand characteristics.

Interval level data

Data measured in fixed units with equal distance between points on the scale

Investigator effects

These result from the effects of a researcher's behavior and characteristics on an investigation.

Laboratory experiment

An experiment that takes place in a controlled environment where the experimenter manipulates the IV and measures the DV

Matched pairs design

An experimental design where pairs of participants are matched on important characteristics and one member allocated to each condition of the IV

Mean

A measure of central tendency calculated by adding all the scores in a set of data together and dividing by the total number of scores

Measures of central tendency

A measurement of data that indicates where the middle of the information lies e.g. mean, median or mode

Median

The measure of central tendency calculated by arranging scores in a set of data from lowest to highest and finding the middle score

Meta-analysis

A technique where rather than conducting new research with participants, the researchers examine the results of several studies that have already been conducted

Mode

The measure of central tendency which is the most frequently occurring score in a set of data

Natural experiment

An experiment where the change in the IV already exists rather than being manipulated by the experimenter

Naturalistic observation

An observation study conducted in an environment where the behavior would normally occur

Negative correlation

A relationship exists between two covariables whereas one increases, the other decreases

Nominal level data

Frequency count data that consists of the number of participants falling into categories. (e.g. 7 people passed their driving test the first time, 6 didn't).

Non-directional hypothesis

A two-tailed hypothesis that does not predict the direction of the difference or relationship (e.g. girls and boys are different in terms of helpfulness).

Normal distribution

An arrangement of a data that is symmetrical and forms a bell-shaped pattern where the mean, median, and mode all fall in the center at the highest peak

Observed value

The value that you have obtained from conducting your statistical test

Observer bias

Occurs when the observers know the aims of the study or the hypotheses and allow this knowledge to influence their observations

Open questions

Questions, where there is no fixed response and participants, can give any answer they like. They generate qualitative data.

Operationalizing variables

This means clearly describing the variables (IV and DV) in terms of how they will be manipulated (IV) or measured (DV).

Opportunity sample

A sampling technique where participants are chosen because they are easily available

Order effects

Order effects can occur in a repeated measures design and refer to how the positioning of tasks influences the outcome e.g. practice effect or boredom effect on the second task

Ordinal level data

Data that is capable of being put into rank order (e.g. places in a beauty contest, or ratings for attractiveness).

Overt observation

Also known as a disclosed observation as the participants given their permission for their behavior to be observed

Participant observation

Observation study where the researcher actually joins the group or takes part in the situation they are observing.

Peer review

Before going to publication, a research report is sent other psychologists who are knowledgeable in the research topic for them to review the study, and check for any problems

Pilot study

A small scale study conducted to ensure the method will work according to plan. If it doesn't then amendments can be made.

Positive correlation

A relationship exists between two covariables whereas one increases, so do the other

Presumptive consent

Asking a group of people from the same target population as the sample whether they would agree to take part in such a study, if yes then presume the sample would

Primary data

Information that the researcher has collected him/herself for a specific purpose e.g. data from an experiment or observation

Prior to general consent

Before participants are recruited they are asked whether they are prepared to take part in research where they might be deceived about the true purpose

Probability

How likely something is to happen – can be expressed as a number (0.5) or a percentage (50% chance of tossing a coin and getting a head)

Protection of participants

Participants should be protected from physical or mental health, including stress - the risk of harm must be no greater than that to which they are exposed in everyday life

Qualitative data

Descriptive information that is expressed in words

Quantitative data

Information that can be measured and written down with numbers.

Quasi-experiment

An experiment often conducted in controlled conditions where the IV simply exists so there can be no random allocation to the conditions

Questionnaire

A set of written questions that participants fill in themselves

Random sampling

A sampling technique where everyone in the target population has an equal chance of being selected

Randomization

Refers to the practice of using chance methods (e.g. flipping a coin' to allocate participants to the conditions of an investigation

Range

The distance between the lowest and the highest value in a set of scores.

Range

A measure of dispersion which involves subtracting the lowest score from the highest score in a set of data

Reliability

Whether something is consistent. In the case of a study, whether it is replicable.

Repeated measures design

An experimental design where each participant takes part in both/all conditions of the IV

Representative sample

A sample that closely matched the target population as a whole in terms of key variables and characteristics

Retrospective consent

Once the true nature of the research has been revealed, participants should be given the right to withdraw their data if they are not happy.

Right to withdraw

Participants should be aware that they can leave the study at any time, even if they have been paid to take part.

Sample

A group of people that are drawn from the target population to take part in a research investigation

Scattergram

Used to plot correlations where each pair of values is plotted against each other to see if there is a relationship between them.

Secondary data

Information that someone else has collected e.g. the work of other psychologists or government statistics

Semi-structured interview

Interview that has some pre-determined questions, but the interviewer can develop others in response to answers given by the participant

Sign test

A statistical test used to analyze the direction of differences of scores between the same or matched pairs of subjects under two experimental conditions

Significance

If the result of a statistical test is significant it is highly unlikely to have occurred by chance

Single-blind control

Participants are not told the true purpose of the research

Skewed distribution

An arrangement of data that is not symmetrical as data is clustered to one end of the distribution

Social desirability bias

Participants' behavior is distorted as they modify this in order to be seen in a positive light.

Standard deviation

A measure of the average spread of scores around the mean. The greater the standard deviation the more spread out the scores are.

Standardized instructions

The instructions given to each participant are kept identical – to help prevent experimenter bias.

Standardized procedures

In every step of the research, all the participants are treated in exactly the same way and so all have the same experience.

Stratified sample

A sampling technique where groups of participants are selected in proportion to their frequency in the target population

Structured interview

Interview where the questions are fixed and the interviewer reads them out and records the responses

Structured observation

An observational study using a predetermined coding scheme to record the participants' behavior

Systematic sample

A sampling technique where every nth person in a list of the target population is selected

Target population

The group that the researchers draws the sample from and wants to be able to generalize the findings to

Temporal validity

Refers to how likely it is that the time period when a study was conducted has influenced the findings and whether they can be generalized to other periods in time

Test-retest reliability

Involves presenting the same participants with the same test or questionnaire on two separate occasions and seeing whether there is a positive correlation between the two

Thematic analysis

A method for analyzing qualitative data which involves identifying, analyzing and reporting patterns within the data

Time sampling

A way of sampling the behavior that is being observed by recording what happens in a series of fixed time intervals.

Type 1 error

It is a false positive. It is where you accept the alternative/experimental hypothesis when it is false

Type 2 error

It is a false negative. It is where you accept the null hypothesis when it is false

Unstructured interview

Also known as a clinical interview, there are no fixed questions just general aims and it is more like a conversation

Unstructured observation

Observation, where there is no checklist so every behavior is seen, is written down in much detail as possible

Validity

Whether something is true – measures what it sets out to measure.

Volunteer sample

A sampling technique where participants put themselves forward to take part in research, often by answering an advertisement

ABOUT THE AUTHOR

Mr. Mubashar Altaf is a lecturer in the Department of English, University of Mianwali. He was born in Pakistan on 02 December 1979. He is MPhil in English literature and Linguistics. He has vast experience in teaching and research. Mubashar is also MSc in Applied Psychology and Masters in Education. He is a teacher, writer, and critic. He has supervised more than twenty research scholars. He has also chaired a session in the first national conference entitled RCELL organized by the University of Sargodha M. B. Din Campus. He has written five books so far.

Lightning Source UK Ltd.
Milton Keynes UK
UKHW011934091021
391942UK00001B/205